Rebuilding the Walls

Rebuilding the Walls

Confronting and Restoring Sin-Damaged Saints

James Kelly

WIPF & STOCK • Eugene, Oregon

REBUILDING THE WALLS
Confronting and Restoring Sin-Damaged Saints

Copyright © 2020 James Kelly. All rights reserved. Except for brief quotations in critical publications or reviews, no part of this book may be reproduced in any manner without prior written permission from the publisher. Write: Permissions, Wipf and Stock Publishers, 199 W. 8th Ave., Suite 3, Eugene, OR 97401.

Wipf & Stock
An Imprint of Wipf and Stock Publishers
199 W. 8th Ave., Suite 3
Eugene, OR 97401

www.wipfandstock.com

PAPERBACK ISBN: 978-1-7252-5677-4
HARDCOVER ISBN: 978-1-7252-5678-1
EBOOK ISBN: 978-1-7252-5679-8

Manufactured in the U.S.A.   06/11/20

To those who refuse to give up on people, who put in the time and effort to seek and save the lost sheep of the flock of God (Luke 15:4). Those workers who faithfully make themselves available to Christ as he builds this spiritual house, with the living stones, his people (1 Pet 2:5).

Contents

     List of Illustrations | viii
     Acknowledgements | ix

Chapter 1 Setting the Stage | 1
Chapter 2 Spiritual Blueprint | 14
Chapter 3 The Balancing Act | 31
Chapter 4 Defining the Problem | 52
Chapter 5 The Restoration Team | 75
Chapter 6 Repairing the Bricks | 86
Chapter 7 Broken Trowel | 102
Chapter 8 Occupancy Permit | 113

Appendix A *BY-LAW 6—Discipline and Restoration* | 123
Appendix B *RCCT Confidentiality Agreement* | 133

     About the Author | 135
     Bibliography | 137

Illustrations

Figure 1   Adam's Diagram | 34
Figure 2   Adjusted Diagram | 35
Figure 3   Adjusted for Leadership Application | 44
Figure 4   Categorization of Sin | 54
Figure 5   Escalation of Financial Sin | 56
Figure 6   Interrelatedness of Sexual Sin | 59
Figure 7   Connectedness of Emotional Sin | 63
Figure 8   Relationship Between Sin in Worship | 66
Figure 9   Development of Cognitive Sin | 69
Figure 10   Common Core of Sinful Activity | 71
Figure 11   Confession Guide | 106

Acknowledgements

I WOULD LIKE TO acknowledge the tireless, dedicated, and selfless service of my wife Christine who assisted me throughout this project. Without her encouragement and assistance, it would not have been completed. I would also like to acknowledge the questions of my children who at times forced me to go back to an area and rethink it. I would also like to thank the Board of Deacons and members of Squamish Community church, who allowed me time away from the office to complete this project. Finally, but definitely not least, I would like to give honor and praise to our wonderful Savior whose amazing grace is abundant and free when we need it the most. To this end a final note, the doxology.

> Praise God, from Whom all blessings flow;
> Praise Him, all creatures here below;
> Praise Him above, ye heav'nly host;
> Praise Father, Son, and Holy Ghost.
> Amen.

Chapter One ⎯⎯⎯⎯⎯⎯⎯⎯⎯⎯⎯⎯⎯⎯⎯⎯⎯⎯⎯⎯⎯⎯

Setting the Stage

SITTING BACKSTAGE IN GLADEWATER, Texas, Johnny Cash penned the words to his famous song, "I Walk The Line." It was his way of spelling out his devotion to his new bride. In a similar fashion, a Christian belts out, "I have decided to follow Jesus, no turning back, no turning back." And yet, the words that Paul wrote to the church in Rome also ring true: "I do not understand what I do. For what I want to do I do not do, but what I hate, I do" (Rom 7.15). Paul continues to expand on this very theme in the verses following, explaining the painful experience of the struggle with sin in the life of a believer. It is to this end that Paul encourages the followers of Christ to be in a constant state of caution regarding sin in their lives. There are times when the saints can correct themselves, working out their sin before the cross and so reflecting the words from Mr. Cash's song not verbally but practically in life. Yet at other times the saints are caught up in their sin and they need the loving assistance of the church to help them out.

In our zeal to rid the church of sin and protect the honor and glory of God, we all too often run over the sinning saint and reduce them to damaged goods that are tarnished in the eyes of the brethren. This is where we need to stop and evaluate how we are administering the discipline of the church, the correction of the saints. There are times where it seems that we have forgotten that we, empowered by the Holy Spirit, are to be about building a people for God. Therefore, to be effective, we need to reconsider exactly how we are dealing with those whose struggle with the sin nature is not going well. What the church needs is a holistic approach to the concept of church discipline where we are presenting an appropriate example of Christ before the world, remembering that the clearest picture of the reality of the face of God that this world can see is in Christ nailed to the cross calling for the forgiveness of those who nailed him there.

In this first chapter we will set forth two concepts as a foundation on which to work. First, the church itself. It is the purpose of this section to provide a definition of the church which will, in turn, provide the conceptual need for the practice of church discipline. There are many who have an understanding of the church that does not allow or accept the possibility of church disciplinary measures. Therefore, we need to have a baseline definition of the church, a clear understanding of what it means to be part of the body of Christ. Second, we need to have an idea of what the biblical motivations for the disciplinary process might look like. A very brief consideration of both preventative and corrective measures will be examined.

Following chapters will examine the procedure or process of discipline, how it needs to start, and the differences between initiating the process in private versus the need for public involvement at the outset of the disciplinary action. From this point, we will then turn to examine those offenses that necessitate being disciplined, taking into consideration that the various lists outlined in Scripture may not be exhaustive and therefore require a discussion of what would necessitate disciplinary activity. The discussion will turn to the examination of the process of restoring those who repent, including what considerations need to come into play to make the restoration process effective for the individual in the given context. Factors that may affect how this restoration program might work are: at what point during the disciplinary process did the individual recognize their sin and respond? What were the specifics of the sin in which the individual was involved? For example, if an individual has been swindling money to cover for a gambling addiction, do both issues need to be considered for any restoration to be productive? This will then frame the final chapter, on restoring the saint to effective fellowship and service within the church.

What is the church?

What is the meaning of a word? In the twenty-first century, we have seen the fluid nature of language possibly as never before in human history. Not only do we have lexicons and dictionaries, but we also have the urban dictionary! Words and phrases have always had some sense of being fluid to the point where the context of what is being said is extremely important to understanding the intent of the speaker. This expands to include cultural boundaries as well. If one were to visit Southeast Asia—India for example—around the Christmas season, one might speak on the topic of the incarnation. However, the point may be missed entirely, as the people there have a theology of incarnation that is vastly different from that of Western Christianity. Therefore, it would be wise to narrow it down to a few concepts to be discussed, to assure that an idea is appropriately communicated. Jay Adams addresses this as the disciplinary process proceeds dealing with a person who appears to be resistant and unrepentant: "you must distinguish carefully between unwillingness to listen and a failure to understand or to accept your viewpoint on the matter."[1] With there being a possibility for misunderstanding a brief look at a communication model might prove helpful to illuminate the possible area where problems could arise.

A simple model of communication has five stages: (1) an idea, (2) the encoding of the idea, (3) the transmission, (4) the decoding of the idea, and, (5) the final idea.[2] The idea is the thought or concept. It may be as simple as "sandwich" or as complex as "the Trinity." Then it is encoded; the two words used to convey these ideas are a good example. Next, there needs to be a mode of transmission, which could be verbal, print, or some other visual medium. The message is received and is decoded by the recipient. Whether the communication was successful is determined by how close the received idea is to that of the original one. This model presents both challenges and solutions to all who engage in attempting to communicate with virtually anyone. The challenges are in the encoding, the transmission, and the decoding of the idea. The individual who wants to share the idea must choose an appropriate method that will convey the idea to the recipient. For example, to transmit an idea in English, in print, would be highly ineffective for someone who speaks only Mandarin and is unable to read. The challenge is expanded when the idea itself may find its expression in both—or either—concrete or conceptual forms. Consider the term "church." Even using what may appear to be clear language in talking about the church/church can be confusing and lead to a fair amount of misunderstanding.

> Part of this misunderstanding results from the multiple usages of the term "church." Sometimes it is used with respect to an architectural structure, a building. Frequently it is used to refer to a particular body of believers; we might, for example, speak of the First Methodist church. At other times, it is used to refer to a denomination, a group set apart by some distinctive; for instance,

1. Adams, *Handbook of Church Discipline*, 58.
2. National Communication Association, "Transactional Model of Communication."

the Presbyterian church or the Lutheran church. In addition to the confusion generated by the multiple usages of the term "church," there is evidence of confusion at a more profound level—a lack of understanding of the basic nature of the church.[3]

Therefore, what we find is that all too often people see the church as a two-thousand-year-old institution or a building. While both definitions are correct, at the same time they may not convey the communicator's intended meaning. Granted, there may be some elements of the church which could resemble a cold dry institution, when in all actuality, it is a living, dynamic entity. This entity, the church, is unique in that its primary purpose is in being a benefit to those who are outside of its influence, those who do not yet know God. Prior to the inception of the church, Christ gave his direction to his followers. They were to go into all the world and make disciples. The term "disciples," meaning the followers of Jesus, are called to go out and teach to establish a community of disciples/learners who can teach. The Greek word for "disciple," specifically in the context of the Great Commission, is μαθητης, which may be translated as "to be a pupil" or "to cause one to be a pupil."[4] Therefore, the purpose of this entity is to create a community based on the concept of learning, and then passing on what is learned.

The core of what must be both taught and understood is that of the redemptive action through the cross, which then may be appropriated by the sinner through the act of faith or trusting God for his salvific provision. So, a sinner becomes a member of the church not through application and acceptance, but through the Spirit of the living God.

> Markus Barth describes baptism as "a comprehensive, practical, public, binding, joyful confession of that 'one faith' in the 'one Lord' which is the beginning of conduct in 'newness of life!' Though a bit more speculative it may be possible to go further and say that we are identified as a member of the body of Christ in the universal sense through Spirit baptism, and we are identified as a member of a local body of Christ through water baptism (see Acts 2:41).[5]

Membership in the body of Christ is a spiritual matter, whereas membership in the local body or church is a matter of identification. Membership in the local church may be resigned or transferred, however an individual maintains their membership in the body of Christ regardless of

3. Erickson, *Christian Theology*, 951.
4. Arndt et al., *Greek-English Lexicon*, 609.
5. Hammet and Merkle, *Those Who Must Give an Account*, 18.

local church affiliation. The Spirit brings people into the universal church however they identify with a local church. This describes membership in the church, not the societies that the church must incorporate with local governments. While this requires a type of membership, it represents only a legal identification with the local body, not necessarily a spiritual connection with the said body. While it may remain a matter of choice as to which local church to join, joining a church is not really an option, as Jonathan Leeman points out: "It's true that a Christian must choose a church, but that does not make it a voluntary organization/choice? Having chosen Christ, a Christian has no choice but to choose to join a church."[6] Therefore, we are incorporated into the universal church, the body of Christ, through our redemption in Christ, but we must, therefore, identify with a local church for the continuing discipleship process. Robert Cheong frames this issue by illustrating the importance of being part of a local church: "We are saved individually to live collectively with others as the bride of Christ."[7] We are called together, to be a people connected to Christ through the cross and to each other through the Spirit, to be a community of faith. This is the Great Commission at work within the people of God, and yet there are still challenges that are faced by both the people of this world and the people of God.

But what challenges could there possibly in fulfilling the Great Commission? People are simply lining up down the street to attend a local church. It almost looks like the first few days when the original Star Wars movie came out: people bartering to get into the church, people moving up and down the lines to scalp tickets to the best seats up in the splash zone, the first few rows. No, wait, that is another reality, not this one. Here, in this reality, the church is a collection of broken people coming together in their brokenness to celebrate the wholeness that is available through the cross of Jesus Christ. The problem is that we never quite become whole on this side of eternity, and while this is frustrating, as we would like to be done with our brokenness and sin, we need to realize just how badly broken we were and still are. The church is sometimes like being in a restaurant, sitting, enjoying a quiet meal, suddenly punctuated by the crashing of a stack of dishes. Granted, in the life of the church, it is not dishes, it is the lives of those with whom we live in fellowship. The crashing is not followed by quiet giggles but by the murmuring of the group, gossip, and backbiting, hidden in the

6. Leeman, *Church Discipline*, 43.
7. Cheong, *God Redeeming His Bride,* 30.

self-righteous language of "sharing prayer requests." "Oh, have you heard the latest? So-and-so certainly needs prayer."

What was just discussed demonstrates two very pertinent illustrations of where church discipline is needed. Firstly, lives are fragile, they get broken, and someone needs to see the need and pick up the pieces. Secondly, those who see the need have to respond in grace and come to the aid of those who are broken. But why the issue of discipline in the church? This group, the church, this gathering of disciples, needs to have a sense of identity to endure. That identity is drawn from its founder and Lord, Jesus Christ. To be like Christ is to be "conformed to the image of His Son" (Rom 8:26). This is part of the journey, namely, being a participant in the church. It is the whole point of becoming Christ-like that is at the heart of the ongoing discipleship process, the mission of the church. The mission of the church is a two-fold discipleship process: the first is, producing disciples (evangelism), and the second is the development or refinement of the disciple (sanctification). It is in the problems that arise in this second stage of the process, the ongoing discipleship of the saint, which we are concerned with here. As noted by Eric Bargerhuff in his book, *Love That Rescues*, "the practice of church discipline is an extension of the Triune God's saving work along the path of authentic discipleship."[8] Therefore, the ongoing refinement of the disciples within the context of the community of faith, the church, is the ongoing activity of God in the refinement of his saints.

At this point, it would help to establish a baseline definition of "the church." As has already been discussed, the church is no mere institution—it is far more. It may have taken a while to get to this point, but in painting a picture it is important to create and layer the background if the foreground is to capture the attention. The descriptions of the church provided in Scripture hint at a greater degree of its dynamic nature. Before addressing some of the descriptions of the church provided in Scripture, we need to understand who makes up this organization. It is one thing to examine the text that refers to the church as the family of God but quite another to understand who makes up the group that is called such. The church is made up of people, not necessarily good or religious people, just people. People from every tribe, nation, tongue, and corner of the world. That sounds like a big church, and it is, the universal church, that is—the universal or catholic church (as is mentioned in the creedal format). The other aspect of the church is the local church, which

---

8. Bargerhuff, *Love That Rescues*, 9.

is the physical representation of the larger body. Membership in both the universal and local church begins with the response to the discipleship process. The response, regardless of the tradition from which we draw our understanding, whether it be predestined, or a free will act, is still the point of entrance into the community which is defined by its trust/faith in the completed work of Christ. It must, therefore, be based on the acknowledgment that one is helpless on one's own, entirely dependent upon the cross. It is this admission and the subsequent submission to the Author and Finisher of one's faith.

The church then is the collection of those affected by the work of the cross, those redeemed by grace, drawn together within the context of the communities in which they live. This lines up with the term used for the church, the εκκλησια, those assembled or gathered together amid our local setting. It has been mentioned in the book, *Those Who Must Give an Account*, that "such a term fits well with the ideas of meaningful, covenanted church membership and the type of accountability reflected in redemptive church discipline."[9] An interesting note is that Hammett and Merkle have looked at the terms which were used to translate terminology into the Septuagint. While this does provide an ideological basis for the use of the terms as they relate to the gathered-together of God, they still reflect a community based on an entirely different relational framework. Thus, entrance into the community of faith, the church, is not based upon the maintaining of a specific code, rather it is based upon the maintaining of a relationship.

Thus, the reality of the church is that it is made up of individual parts that are the church and at the same time only one part of the church. Robert Cheong commented on this by stating that "we are saved individually to live collectively with others as the bride of Christ."[10] A single entity made of many parts. It cannot be properly defined by either. While it is the whole, that does not explain the nature of the whole. At the same time, the many parts are not entirely sufficient to reflect the reality of the whole. In this sense, the mystery of the Trinity is reflected in the church. The Holy Trinity both reflects the singular reality while acknowledging the triune structure of the God it attempts to define, the impossible theological math problem ($1 + 1 + 1 = 1$). Then we have the church where the specific integers, which are added together, are too numerous to count and yet still reflect the sum, 1—the church, universal/catholic/invisible,

---

9. Hammett and Merkle, *Those Who Must Give an Account*, 11.
10. Cheong, *God Redeeming His Bride*, 30.

while at the same time is local and identifiable. The text of Scripture provides several pictures of the church: the body of Christ (1 Cor 12:27), the bride of Christ (2 Cor 11:2), the temple of the Holy Spirit (1 Cor 3:16), and the people of God (2 Cor 6:16). While this list is not entirely exhaustive, it does illustrate the nature of the church. If it would be necessary to identify and hold to one definition or picture that characterizes the church, it might be prudent to consider the recipient of Luke's works, Theophilus. To whomever Luke was writing, the name/title provided here certainly provides the best characterization of the church, as this term may be translated as "lover of God."[11] Another possible translation could be "loved by God." Both would be easily applicable to the church. Thus, as a working or baseline characterization of the church, we have people, who are both loved of God and lovers of God, while at the same time engaged in lives that are both broken by and continue to be broken by sin.

With this being the case, the nature of the church is reflected both in the invisible universal church as well as the local church. It is, however, visible through both in the lives of the individuals that make up the church and the collective community itself. How one lives reflects how the world views the nature of the church—which brings into tension the two parallel realities of the church, namely, the fact that, while the church is redeemed, it is made up of sinners, saved by grace, but sinners none the less. The tension noted in the Latin phrase "*simul iustus et peccator,*" translates "at the same time righteous and sinner." It is to answer this tension that Christ gave us the model of church discipline as outlined in Matt 18:15–20. When the saint falls back into the practice of the sinner, there is a problem as the saint no longer reflects the nature of the church that is being conformed to the image of Christ. Gordon Fee discusses the nature of this tension with the phrase "already/not yet." The saint is caught in the tension of the transformation of living life according to the Spirit (κατα πνευμα) and departing from living life according to the flesh (κατα σαρκα).

It is concerning this tension that Paul refers to as spiritual warfare, the weapons of which are: the helmet of salvation, the breastplate of righteousness, the shield of faith, the belt of the truth, feet shod with the preparation of the gospel, and the sword of the Spirit (Eph 6:13–17). The battle that we fight is internal as Paul has illustrated in Rom 7:14–20. What I so fondly refer to as the "do do" verses. Why? Because they reflect how we so instinctually get our lives in deep "do do." The things that we do want to

---

11. Zodhiates, *Complete Word Study Dictionary.*

do (those actions and attitudes that reflect *iustus* and living κατα πνευμα), are continually offset by those things that we actually do do (those actions and attitudes that reflect *peccator* and living κατα σαρκα), the things that as members of the redeemed community we do not want to do. Yet these things we actually keep doing, much to our disgrace and frustration. It is to this end that these verses are affectionately called the "do do" verses because they reflect the amount of "do do" in our lives.

What is Church Discipline?

So, if we accept that the church is a collection of people who are defined as those who love God and are loved of God, then what exactly do we do when actions, attitudes, and beliefs come into contrast with that of God's design? The whole point of the Law and the gospel is people learning to live in relationship with God. While this is the whole point of everything—creation, the Law, the gospel, that is, living in relationship with God—it is at the same time the problem. The very makeup and nature of man, at least since the fall, is that everything is egocentric.[12] While the entire structure of the Law is meant to recognize this problem, man looking into the perfect Law of God missed the point entirely. Instead of understanding that fulfilling the Law was impossible for fallen sinful man, man then tried all the harder to live up to the requirements of the Law throwing disdain on those who were unable to live up to their standards even while the best of man could not live up to the standards of a holy, righteous God!

Therefore, the problem is that the church, this entity that is so loved by God, falls so short of being what God called and intended it to be. The lives of those who make up this entity, regardless of its application, invisible or visible, are pursued by the God who loves them, similar to Hosea's pursuit of Gomer. Consider this: Hosea, a man of God, is called of God to marry a "promiscuous woman and have children with her" (Hos 1:2c)! She is identified in other translations as "a wife of harlotry"[13] or "a wife of whoredom."[14]

---

12. Dr. Susan Whitbourne has commented in an article published on the *Psychology Today* website that egotism is that natural restriction on our perception caused by the simple fact that we can only see the world from our own perspective. Further to the point, Dr. Whitbourne comments that it requires special effort to perceive the world through anything but our own perspective (Whitbourne, "It's a Fine Line").

13. NASB and NKJV.

14. NRSV and ESV.

The point is not that Hosea was a heroic individual in a matrimonial setting, but that God was the hero in a relational setting with man. Hosea's courting and the pursuit of Gomer was, and still is to this day, a living illustration of God's pursuit of sinful man. This is what church discipline is: God pursuing man as man wallows in the depths of sin. As a baseline definition is considered for the concept of church discipline, this definition will consider the various levels or layers of church discipline.

Church discipline is God reaching out to his people, to his people in a similar act of redemption to that of the initial salvation. While initial salvation is the result of the Great Commission and Great Commandments being directed toward the unregenerate life, church discipline is the same directed towards those who have already encountered Christ and yet have become lost in sin again. Those who are lost again in sin are not lost as the church would normally consider an individual to be lost, but they have lost their way in Christ due to the blinding power of sin. The blinders fall off through the activity of the Holy Spirit reaching into the lives of those so affected (Acts 9:18). This activity, as previously noted has multiple levels or layers. These layers of ministry in this area begin with being both preventative and corrective. Carl Laney recognizes this pattern in his book, *A Guide to Church Discipline*: "In Eph. 6:4, Paul recognizes two major types of discipline which parents are given authority to administer: (1) training by act (discipline), and (2) training by word (instruction)."[15] Discipline, the corrective action, is required when instruction, the preventive method, is not effective in a specific situation. This is still God's redemptive work in the lives of people. It is towards this end that Eric Bargerhuff notes, "the practice of church discipline is an extension of the Triune God's saving work along the path of authentic discipleship."[16] God disciplines those who are his own as an extension of his saving grace: ergo grace does not end at the individual's conversion, it continues to draw the individual to God through the cross. The difference is that discipline is a reminder of the individual's place in God through the cross. If we consider Bargerhuff's statement above, then it may be rightfully deduced that church discipline is an extension of evangelism or sharing the good news with the redeemed.

---

15. Laney, *A Guide to Church Discipline*, 29.
16. Bargerhuff, *Love That Rescues*, 9.

Prevention

This act of grace, the working out of the evangelistic endeavor as it is expressed in the lives of believers/the redeemed, begins with the process outlined in the Great Commission. The process of discipling never really ends on this side of eternity. That is God is never finished with us until such a time that we are gathered into his presence. As long as we are in this struggle we need to deal with the ever-present sinful nature in our lives. The first level of discipline in the church is through preventative measures. This begins both at the pulpit and in the classroom in the church, although it hardly ends at these levels.

People do not come into the church with an understanding of the various spiritual disciplines, such as silence, solitude, or meditation. If they do have a basic concept of these disciplines, their understanding will most likely reflect more of the influence of the world than a biblically based spiritual discipline. The instruction in the spiritual disciplines should take place in the context of a "pastor's class" or new believers' class. The practice of the disciplines can be put in place in the life of a believer, factors that will prevent some sinful practices from developing—similar to a speed bump on a roadway causing a driver to slow down and possibly avoid an accident. There are several passages that speak to this point, building up oneself in the Spirit or to specifically take stock of one's life to measure spiritual growth (Phil 2:12; 1 Cor 11:28; 2 Cor 13:5; Heb 3:13; 2 Pet 1:5–9). Even though well-taught spiritual disciplines can be implemented in the lives of believers, the sin nature is still there. While these practices can assist a believer in being aware of encroaching sin, they cannot eliminate it. This will be discussed in a later chapter as the implementation of some of these disciplines will play a role in the restoration of the stumbling saint.

Correction

The preventative side of the disciplinary process has at its core several methodologies to become aware of sin crouching at the door. Yet sin at times still gets in and causes all sorts of sorrow and hardship for saints who are trying to live out their faith. All too often in the process of correction (discipline), it is the sinning saint that is attacked rather than the sin that they are engaged in. This is a serious problem, possibly as serious as the sin itself. While the process of corrective discipline will be examined later, at this point what is necessary is to take a closer look at the purpose and motivation behind the action. The disciplinary activities of the church must never be undertaken or viewed from a punitive perspective. The actions of the church in disciplining its members must reflect the redemptive nature of the gospel.

> . . . the idea of divine discipline is woven so deeply and intricately into the very identity, redemptive stories, and personal experiences of the people of God in covenant with Yahweh. It is a prominent part of the story of redemption. It is part of God's design to handle the problem of sin for His people to know and love Him and follow Him and His commands while recognizing His holy sovereign rule over them and the world.[17]

It is not about punishment; rather, it is about redemption, correction, and restoration. This is deliberately an act of the grace of God. As Mark Lauterbach so eloquently put it: "Grace disciplines."[18] While this may seem to be an overly simplistic issue to bring to the discussion, it is all too often forgotten or ignored. This is where the problems begin, where those in leadership are either too aggressive in their handling of the situation or they are too complacent. Either way, neither grace nor love is being effectively reflected in the situation.

There are two different positions to consider at this point. The first is the protection of the name and glory of God, the second is the restoration of the saint. Now the issue of protecting the name and glory of God needs a little unpacking. In speaking to the prophet Jeremiah, God declares that the people of Israel and Judah were to be for his "renown, praise and honor" (Jer 13:11). That is, a people called to be his, a holy nation (Exod 16:9), a priesthood for God's purposes. Peter mentions that they are to be God's "special possession" (1 Pet 2:9). The call of God is not entirely for the benefit of fallen man, as God has also called man for his purposes, and for his name's sake. Thus, when those who are called by him fail to live in a way that pleases God, that dishonors his name. While the Law in the Old Testament may have had punitive measures[19] in place, in the covenant of grace the goal is to

---

17. Bargerhuff, *Love That Rescues*, 76.

18. Lauterbach, *The Transforming Community*, 58.

19. The stipulations of the law may be seen as either punitive in punishing the sinner or as an act of purging the sin from the midst of the people of God, much like the practice of the Feast of Unleavened Bread. The removing of the impurities from the nation of Israel, the people of God. Leaven is often used in the Scriptures as an illustration of sin. The most effective way of dealing with leaven/sin is to completely remove it.

restore those who have fallen into sin. Under grace, it is not the sinner that is necessarily removed but the sin, and it is only when the sinner refuses to forsake the sin that the sinner is removed. It is towards this end that the practice of church discipline is aimed.

Summing up this chapter, the church has been defined and the discussion has considered two primary approaches to church discipline both preventive and corrective. The church has been identified as a unique entity. It is not just an organization and it is far more than a building. The church is a collection of people, individuals with different ideas, skills, gifts, and abilities who are gathered together by the Spirit to be the physical representation of God on earth until such a time that his work among humanity is completed. This gathering is all too often marred by the very fact that mankind is broken, not by accident but by deliberate disobedience (Gen 3:1–11; Rom 5:12). Even the application of the gifts which are given through the Spirit can be affected by the brokenness/fallenness of the gifted person. Not the gift of God, but the application of the gift, it was to this end that Paul had to place restrictions on the use of the grace gifts in the church in Corinth (1 Cor 14:22–25). This text is a form of church discipline as Paul, through teaching, corrected the church in its application of the gifts.

Different situations require different approaches. Not every situation is the same, sin is still sin, but the confrontation of that sin and the restoring of the sinner is not always the same. To this end, we have been given by the head of the church various illustrations of how we are to go about the confrontation and disciplining of those who are engaged in sin. The preventative and corrective measures are seen in the section of Paul's letter to the church in Corinth. It does deal with an existing problem, the abuse of the gift of tongues (corrective), while at the same time, if his words are heeded it deals with possible future abuse (preventative) (1 Cor 14). We have in the text of Scripture a number of paradigms of how to deal with sin in the church, this on the corrective end. As we will see in the next chapter two primary factors in determining the process of confrontation are public knowledge of the offense and the response of the offender.

Chapter Two _____

Scriptural Blueprints

IN THE SCRIPTURES, we find several models for the disciplinary process, some of which appear more involved than others. Each contains unique elements that require investigation for determining the context in which they are found and thus how they might potentially be applied today. For example, there are situations where the application of one model may either be too heavy-handed or too gentle for the sin that is involved. Additionally, there are very real differences between publicly known sins, sins that are private between two people, or cases where those in leadership have been caught in sin.

In this chapter I will make a careful examination of the various texts dealing with a saint who is caught in sin, followed by a discussion of how these texts might be applied in a contemporary setting with people who live messy lives within the church.[1]

Three specific texts will be discussed here, the order of which will be according to the complexity of the process in approaching the sinning saint. While there is nothing contradictory in the various models that will be examined, understanding the context is essential in understanding the application for each situation. Has it remained a private matter that those in the church have discovered in some way, or is this public and already well-known in a more public forum? To bring the chapter to a close, I will examine the idea in Scripture of "covering over sin." Twice in the Old Testament—specifically in the book of Proverbs—and once in the New Testament in Peter's first letter, it is clearly stated that "love covers" over an offense or sin (Prov 10:12, 17:9; 1 Pet 4:8). While from a strictly theological perspective only the cross can wash away sin's stain, I will explore the texts

---

1. The reason that the discussion will deal with those inside the church is that Paul has noted that we have no business to judge those outside the church (1 Cor 5:12–13).

in view to see if there is any sense in which this love can truly cover over a trespass—and, if so, to what end?

Matt 18:15–17 (NIV)

As we begin to examine this text, we are faced with a translation problem: not all translations agree about the first verse. The NIV and the NASB both read as "if your brother (NIV: or sister) sins" whereas the ESV, the NKJV, and the Message all include the phrase "against you." Who then should approach the sinning saint first? Both the NIV and NASB seem to suggest anyone who has discovered the sinful activity should approach the sinning saint. The other three versions seem to place the emphasis on the individual against whom the sin is directed or has been affected by the sin. The difference comes down to the handling of the Greek "εις σε." Does this translate the "against you" or is this an imposition of an external idea on the text?

The Greek "εις σε" is, according to Metzger, one of the textual anomalies concerning this section of text.[2] Metzger is not clear on whether the problem is due to the section being added after the fact, omitted, or if it was deliberate or accidental. What is in question here is the expansion of the core of the text. While it really does not impact the core theology of the passage, the need for confrontation, the omission of the phrase does suggest a more generalized approach to the issue of sin. As the discussion continues through to v. 20, according to Metzger, it appears that the preferred reading would be the omission of the phrase, due to its uncertain origin, thereby making the overall reading more generalized. Therefore, anyone in the church who discovers a brother in sin has the right and/or the responsibility to approach, confront, and rebuke that individual.

Commentators also note that the inclusion of this phrase "unhelpfully restricts the scope"[3]—that is, the sin is not personally affecting the third person involved, but as a matter of responsibility to a brother in the faith, challenges the saint who is sinning for the sinning saint's own spiritual well-being. It has been suggested that the issue has a homophonic origin.[4] While this has been an issue on the copying of texts over the course of time, the plausibility seems questionable as there does not seem to be any term within close proximity that sounds similar, and therefore must be the

---

2. Metzger, *Textual Commentary*, 36.
3. France, "Matthew," 928.
4. Blomberg, *Matthew*, 278.

source. The point is that the general sense of responsibility for the spirituality of a brother or sister in the faith should not be set aside based on a portion of the text around which there are questions.

This section appears to be dealing with private offenses that are not public knowledge, since Christ instructs those who do know of the offense to deal with it privately, at least at the outset. As the process continues forward, it is the resistance of the offender that determines the amount of publicity that the issue receives. It seems clear that the issue at hand is responding to the spiritual injury of a fellow member of the community of faith. Its focus is not to publicly humiliate, but to bring the person back into the depth of fellowship that the individual once enjoyed with God. This is illustrated in the escalating action when there is no response to the call back into fellowship with the church and God. It is possible that the inclusion of the disputed phrase relates to this very point, making the intention to keep it personal/private. Therefore, only those with a personal connection to the offense may address the issue with the offender. It is only as the offender's heart is hardened—or proven to be hard that the scope of those who are aware of the offense increases.

The text is concerned with the continuation of the process if, and only if, a person is unsuccessful in turning the brother/sister from sin. One point brought up by a commentator is that the individual may not even realize that they have sinned, thus bringing it to their attention in a private manner gives the individual a chance to catch themselves and correct the issue.[5] The intended result that Christ has is to see the person respond, as the NIV puts it, "you have won your brother over," that is, grace wins (Matt 18:15e). This is emphasized in the *New Bible Commentary*: "The aim must be to win your brother over, restoration, not punishment. To that end, the minimum of publicity must be used."[6] In protecting the individual who is caught in sin, from public knowledge, it may be that the individual is being protected in a sense from themselves and their own short-sightedness.

The final phase of the disciplinary process as outlined here is the public rebuke which, if unsuccessful, will lead to a change in the status of that individual regarding the assembly. The unrepentant individual was to be treated as one who was outside the covenant community. Neither the pagan nor tax collector were to be considered as individuals with whom those in the community would have close personal contact. However, this is an

---

5. Wiersbe, *Bible Exposition Commentary*, vol. 1, 65.
6. France, "Matthew," 928.

instruction that has come directly from Jesus Christ, himself, the friend of sinners. The treatment of the offender as a pagan or a tax collector is to make it crystal clear that they are no longer living according to the standards of the covenant community. While this is true, the individual is not to be treated with contempt. Being recognized as one outside the community, they are now the object of the evangelical phase of the discipleship process. The Lord Jesus, himself stated that he came to seek and save that which was lost. While we understand that this is primarily directed at those who have yet to enter into the community of faith, those who through sin are stepping away from the fellowship of the saints would certainly fall into the category of "the lost." In this passage, Jesus is not speaking to the erring saint but rather to those offended, or those in the community of faith who have become aware of their brother or sister's error. It is their conduct that is outlined here. Those who recognize sin in the community need to reach out to those who wander, as ambassadors of the kingdom, imploring them to be reconciled to God. As observant members of the community of faith, they are to be obedient to God. This point is outlined by Warren Wiersbe when he states, "Our attitude should not be that of a policeman out to arrest a criminal, but rather that of a physician seeking to heal a wound in the body of Christ, a wound that will spread sickness and death if left alone."[7] The instruction is clear: deal with those caught in sin. The motive may be a little harder to grasp, responding in grace, not just sanctimonious indignation, but the focus is to rescue the fallen. This would fit with the mission of the church as laid out through the Great Commission (Matt 28:19–20) and the Great Commandment (Matt 22:37–39). Therefore, while the pronouncement upon the unrepentant sounds harsh, it may be little more than a colloquial phrase identifying those outside the community of faith.

Titus 3:9–11 (NIV)

In Titus 3:9–11 Paul's focus is on false teaching, but the exact nature of what is being taught or shared is not specified. Paul instructs his readers to avoid "foolish controversies and genealogies and arguments and quarrels about the law" (3:9). The point that Paul makes is that these discussions can become divisive, causing disruption within the body, the membership. To put this into a different perspective, consider the debate at the very first church conference in Jerusalem. From the report in Scripture, it wrapped up well, however, we

---

7. Wiersbe, *Wiersbe's Expository Outlines*, 68–69.

are not given every detail concerning the conference (Acts 15:1–35). We are told that it was dealing with at least one contentious issue, that of Gentiles and circumcision. While not every encounter ends as well as it seems the Jerusalem conference did, the church must still deal with issues that arise often with members who have strongly held positions.

In this text, Paul has a somewhat different approach to sin in comparison to that which was laid out by Jesus in Matthew. The most significant difference is the number of attempts made to turn the individual from their error. While Christ narrates three attempts, Paul here only sets out two attempts. The public nature of this matter is at the heart of the variance in the approach. All too often the issues in the text of Scripture are understood entirely from a contemporary perspective, rather than in the setting where and when they actually took place. Therefore, when considering the possibility of a private sin such as is the subject of Matt 18, it could very well be a well-concealed issue. Now, in contrast, is the issue here in Titus, one that is essentially of a more public nature. Considering the proximity and nature of urban living: a person's business was literally everyone's business.

Paul's discussion in ch. 3 is basically soteriological in nature with the focus on the present effects of being in a relationship with God. His discussion turns to a disciplinary issue when bringing to light those who unnecessarily initiate contentious discussions that have little to no value for those with whom they are engaging. The key term here is found in v. 10, translated in the NIV as a "divisive person" from the Greek term "αιρετικον"—*airew* which translates as "one who creates or fosters factions,"[8] "as to pertaining to the causing of divisions."[9] Other sources add the fact that this term has been used to describe "heretical persons."[10] The idea behind the term is that of a person who is intent on causing problems within the unity of a group. It is not just a person with different ideas, rather this must be understood as someone who is deliberately causing problems in the church. The Greek conveys a greater sense of the severity of this offense than English versions do, therefore the Greek needs to be brought into consideration at this point. This identifies a single person as the source of unproductive doctrine/contention. While there may be more than one person who has been disseminating it, the text seems to suggest a singular point of origin.

8. Wigram, *Analytical Greek Lexicon*, 9.
9. Arndt et al., *Greek-English Lexicon*, 28.
10. Liddell and Scott, *Greek-English Lexicon*, 41.

The terminology, from which the English term "heretic" is derived, places a great deal of emphasis on the person rather than on the actual concept or doctrine that is being taught. A heretic is defined by Warren Wiersbe as "one who makes a choice, who causes division."[11] These are individuals who, it would seem, are not so much interested in the spread of the gospel, or those who are in Christ becoming more deeply grounded in the faith; rather, their purpose appears to spread what might promote themselves or cause contention.[12] Consequently, the only truly safe conclusion is that while we may not be able to determine what these divisive people were teaching, it was concerning doctrinal issues that were in conflict with the gospel message.

The directive provided by Paul is not the correction of the doctrine of those divisive people but the correction of the people themselves. Donald Guthrie points this out: " . . . he draws a distinction between the teaching and the people involved."[13] Paul does not direct Titus or the church to chase the symptoms but rather to deal with the cause. Ultimately, this is an issue that needs to be corrected, Paul leaves no uncertainty here. But Paul's directive is not to address the false teaching, rather "having nothing to do with them" indicates Paul's concern is with the teachers. While the emphasis within the text may seem to be a hard line against these individuals, the point is still to rebuke and call them back (Gal 6:1). Paul's instructions are, "Warn a divisive person once, and then warn them a second time" (3:10a). This follows the pattern laid out beginning in Matthew with the teaching directly from Christ. While the passage here seems to jump a step, rather than three warnings Paul here states two. The possibility of only two warnings or confrontations is due to the public nature of the offense. The importance of dealing with erroneous teaching is clearly laid out by Paul. In both vv. 10 and 11, he lays out a clear emphasis on the need to correct and the need to reject those who will not be corrected. Paul goes so far as to say these people are "self-condemned" (3:11).

---

11. Wiersbe, *Bible Exposition Commentary*, vol. 2, 268.

12. There are some commentators that suggest that these "heretics" are Judaizers and therefore present a threat to the gospel message. While this specific text is directed to Titus in Crete, a Gentile leading the church there, there is no direct evidence concerning the origin of the church in Crete within the text of Scripture. Therefore, we have no real evidence suggesting the cultural backgrounds of the congregation. It is these facts that raise questions concerning the conclusion that the heretics where Judaizers.

13. Guthrie, "Titus," in Carson et al., *New Bible Commentary*, 1311–15.

Therefore, as with the text in Matthew, the point is to confront and turn the teacher from the direction that they are heading in. It is important for every pastor and Christian to be concerned with people, especially those who are causing problems or struggling in regard to issues of faith. The double warning here seems to be in keeping with the framework provided by Christ in Matthew. The matter is already publicly known, and therefore, any initial step done privately is no longer relevant. The fact that these people fuel dissensions and factions (Gal 5:20), disrupting the life of the body of Christ, is enough to demand that action be taken to address them. Guthrie points out that it appears that Paul feels that individuals of this type are of a warped mind and therefore it is highly unlikely that they might respond beyond the two confrontations.[14] Should these individuals not be confronted the result would be a divided church that is ineffective in reaching the lost for Christ.

1 Cor 5:1–5 (NIV)

This text addresses several very disturbing issues. Paul states that he has heard the report that a man is in an intimate relationship with his father's wife. First and foremost, that this situation even exists is appalling. What we are not directly told, however, is the exact nature of this relationship. Robertson Nicol comments that the depravity being exercised by this individual is a "sin of unparalleled blackness."[15] While this should be enough of a rebuke, there is yet more, in that it seems that this is somewhat public knowledge. The situation that Paul is addressing here has gone beyond the confines of the church in Corinth—it has even reached his ears in Ephesus (1 Cor 16:8, 19)! How this reached Paul's ears being some 350 miles (570 km) from where the event took place is another problem. The text states that "it is actually reported" (5:1), not that they had deliberately or directly reported it to Paul or inquired about what to do with the situation. The situation had come to Paul's attention through some other format, concerning which, commentators are silent. All that the text reads concerning this matter is, "It is actually reported that there is . . . " (5:1). Paul names no source nor does he record whether this was word of mouth or written: he simply states, it is "reported." This is unfortunate, as it speaks to the sequence that Paul commands the church to follow in dealing with the situation. A variant

---

14. Guthrie, "Titus," 1315.
15. Nicoll, *Expositor's Greek Testament: Commentary*, vol. 2, 807.

reading of the text from the Greek would be "everyone has heard" thereby suggesting that a much larger group of people are aware of the situation. This speaks directly to the course of action that Paul strongly suggests the church take, which is dependent on two crucial points.

The first point is the nature of the offense: and the second point is the public's awareness of the offense. As mentioned previously, this is an offense of unparalleled blackness, or, putting it another way, this sin was so gross that the heathen avoids it.[16] While the text is not clear as to the identity of either person, it appears that the male is a member of the church in Corinth. Some commentators have put forward the suggestion that the woman involved was not a Christian.[17] The basis for this proposition is that Paul at no time suggests that the woman is included in the discipline, which is directed towards the man. Granted, this is hardly conclusive, but the article in Greek is in the masculine form, and traditionally, the initiation of sexual interaction has been placed on the male. Consider the restriction in the Mosaic legal structure from Leviticus (18:8) and Deuteronomy (22:30; 27:20) and compare this to Solomon's comments in the Proverbs concerning the wayward woman (Prov 7).[18]

The relationship may not have been incestuous, as there is no evidence to support that, but this individual was in an intimate relationship with his mother. The text only states that he was with his father's wife. This could have been a stepmother, or, if the individual's father had multiple wives, it could have been any one of a number of stepmothers. While this does not change the nature of the offense, it may cause a shift in our thinking. A reader may view this text with the presupposition that this is a relationship between a mother and son, which is unlikely. In such an event Paul would certainly have addressed the situation as such. Thus, the only likely determination is that the woman in this situation was a wife or former wife of the individual's father, yet not his mother. If the man's father were still alive and married to the woman, Paul again would have certainly referred to such a relationship as adultery. To accept this in no way legitimizes the situation because, as Paul has pointed out, it is unacceptable even in pagan circles. As

---

16. Jamieson et al., *Commentary Critical and Explanatory*, vol. 2, 271.

17. Barrett, *First Epistle to the Corinthians*.

18. If we consider the legal passages, then the man is the one who bears the sole responsibility in the interaction. If, however, we bring the comments from Proverbs into the equation, then the woman may also bear a certain amount of responsibility and thus be included in the discipline.

David Lowery notes, Roman law forbade such relationships,[19] although the two individuals may not even have been related in any other way.

The fact that the two were engaged in a relationship, and that this was a public spectacle, is at the heart of the issue. The sin that is addressed in Matthew—and we are not told what the sin there was—this hypothetical construct is such that it provides a universal paradigm for dealing with sin within the context of the people of God. The point is that there was sin and that it was dealt with through the various stages, moving from private to public in the scope of those knowing about it. Whereas, here, in Paul's letter to Corinth, the matter is already public and therefore demands swift attention (1 Cor 5:2). Paul is adamant that this issue needs to be dealt with swiftly and decisively. He declares that even in his absence that he has pronounced judgment on the individual involved. Also, there is a bit of ambiguity as the Greek article here, in v. 2, is in the singular masculine form and may be referring to the situation or couple rather than the male individual. It is dangerous to read too much into the text when the language isn't entirely specific! If the woman was not a Christian/a member of the community of faith, then the reference would be to the man alone. However, if the woman was a member of the community of faith, then there are problems with what appears to be a traditional reading of the text. Regardless, the outcome must be understood that under certain circumstances a disciplinary response from the church must be swift, clear, and decisive, that those involved in sin must be dealt with, and, depending on the amount of public knowledge of the offense, how it should be dealt with and who should be dealt with. Sin cannot remain in the church, as in the case of Achan and the defeat at Ai (Josh 7:1–26; 22:20); if sin remains then the people of God cannot move forward in triumph.

Matt 18:18–20 (NIV)

What does it mean to "hold the keys to heaven?" One point that must be established at the outset of this part of the discussion is that the authority for binding and loosing resides with the Sovereign King. The activity that is undertaken by the church must follow the direction provided in Scripture. This is not a matter for wielding inappropriate control. The text, according to Blomberg, is presupposing that the church will be "acting in accordance with Jesus' guidelines" from the previous passages, and when

---

19. Lowery, "1 Corinthians," 514.

doing so, the church is the expression of God's authority on earth.[20] All too often this passage is taken out of context with people interpreting it as a reference to the granting of requests. This passage, however, is a reflection of the spiritually-led judicial process dealing with people in their struggle with sin and grace. Thus, the presence of the Lord in the gathering of the saints is in direct relation to the process of discipline. When dealing with difficult issues and having to pronounce certain courses of action, having the knowledge of God's presence is the reassurance that is at times necessary to move forward.

This is a similar passage to that found earlier in Matthew (16:19) where Jesus is talking to Peter, the context again being the building of the church. The declaration from this text is that Christ will build his church and that Peter will have a certain amount of authority concerning those who could have entered into the church. Blomberg connects this passage to God giving the same authority to Eliakim, of whom we know very little.[21] It is suggested that he was a palace administrator, possibly of a priestly line, yet it is with this man that God places the key to opening and closing the way. In a similar fashion to the authority being removed from Shebna and given over to Eliakim (Isa 22:20–25), the authority of administrating the people of God under the new covenant is transferred from the priesthood and the temple to those assigned by God to be apostles, prophets, evangelists, teachers, and pastors (Eph 4:11). The purpose of these assignments is to prepare people for service, to build unity, and to grow in Christ. The very presence of sin is diametrically opposed to this growth and must, therefore, be dealt with.

In giving the keys to the kingdom to Peter, Christ was empowering Peter with the role of steward over the affairs of the church, not as a singular individual, but symbolically for all those in the community of faith. Spurgeon made the point, "When those keys are rightly turned by the assembly below, the act is ratified above: that which they bind on earth shall be bound in heaven."[22] The point is not that the church or any member of the church controls these "keys" but rather when the church is keeping to the Word of God, it is exercising the will of God and thus "rightly turning" the keys. The result is the binding and loosing of the saints. The question then is, "to what extent is the saint bound or loosed"? Accepting the fact that by following the

---

20. Blomberg, *Matthew*, 280.
21. Beale and Carson, *Commentary on the New Testament*, 55.
22. Spurgeon, *Gospel of the Kingdom*, 153.

procedures laid down by God in his word, by Christ in Matthew, and by Paul in both Titus and 1 Corinthians, it is not then the church that is binding or loosing, but as the church is led by the Spirit, it is the Spirit of God doing so. The church, in carrying out the instructions of the Lord, allows the erring saint to see themselves reflected in the mirror of the word.

Gal 6:1–5 (NIV)

Paul, in his letter to the church in Galatia, reinforces the point that when it comes to the issue of church discipline the purpose is to restore the people of God who struggle with sin. Timothy George states that understanding this point is extremely important to understanding the purpose of congregational discipline. The purpose is to correct and restore the erring saint to the fellowship of believers. This is extended not only to the clergy—to those in leadership positions—but to every member of a given assembly of saints. The truly spiritual are not those who lord it over a saint who has fallen into sin; rather, the mark of the spiritual man is restoring the fallen. There is in the text a clear contrast between those who are pious and those who are spiritual. The Pharisees of Paul's day had a sense of self-appointed spirituality and yet they did little for those in their community who struggled with sin but would contrast themselves against such for their own glory (Luke 18:11–14). However, Paul wanted those in the church in Galatia to understand that sin was a disruption to fellowship with the Lord and the church.

The address here, "for those who are spiritual," is not an attempt to create a new sect of Pharisees in the Christian church; rather, he was pointing out that those who truly walk in the Spirit—or are spiritually led—will seek to help the brother or sister in error. The love that is the evidence of the Spirit seeks to put the needs of the brother above their own. If we look back to Cain's questioning response to God concerning Abel, "Am I my brother's keeper?" the answer is an overwhelming "yes!" To this point, George Timothy states: "Those who are spiritually minded, that is, those whose lives give evidence of the fruit of the Spirit, have a special responsibility to take the initiative in seeking restoration and reconciliation with those who have been caught in such an error."[23] The idea is that those who are in an active and dynamic relationship with Christ assist those who struggle with sin, even if the offender has been in Christ longer or has greater knowledge. Those who

---

23. George, *Galatians*, 410.

are found in the Spirit are to be the support and strength that is needed by the ones who may be (even if just temporarily) weaker.

Paul's instruction is to restore the offender "gently" or "with a spirit of gentleness."[24] It is painfully true that anyone can fall into temptation and then teeter into sin. No one is immune from the reality that even after we encounter the living God through grace, we are still susceptible to sin. It is to this point that John informs us that anyone who thinks that they are free from sin is deceived (1 John 1:8). For many, possibly even those who may be considered spiritual, they may find themselves in sin and then need to deal with it appropriately before the cross of Christ (1 John 1:9). These are those who most likely while understanding their own propensity to sin, are able to turn and extend the grace of God into the life of an erring brother or sister and journey with them.

Some of the discussions concerning this verse focus on the conditions under which this sin has occurred. The English translations seem to convey an individual who has been discovered to be engaged in some form of sinful activity. While there is a sense in the Greek that this is an individual who has literally been caught with his "hand in the cookie jar," there is also support to suggest that this is an individual who has been overtaken by sin. The saint was not looking to sin, they may have been exposed to a specific temptation so hard and so fast that they were unable to avoid it.[25] As the text describes "caught in sin," the idea of an individual engaging in deliberate sin would need to be balanced against the text in Heb 10:26—the deliberate or willful, that is, a full defection from the faith. That is not so much an occurrence into a sinful practice or even the repeated indulgence into sin, but the abandonment of the life of faith in Christ; the saint who gives into sin rather than struggling against it.

1 Cor 5:9–13 (NIV)

It is apparent from the wording in this passage that 1 Corinthians is not the first letter that Paul wrote to the church in Corinth. It is, however, the first letter that has been included in the text of the canon. While the possibility of a previous letter has little impact on the current message, suffice it to say that this was an issue that had been previously discussed and that there

---

24. Silva, "Galatians," in Carson et al., *New Bible Commentary*, 1206–21.
25. Rendall, "Epistle of Paul to the Galatians," in Nicoll, *The Expositor's Greek Testament*, vol. 3, 188. Also, Stutzman, *Exegetical Summary of Galatians*, 231.

was some clarification required. The point that needed to be revisited had to do with the treatment of those who were engaging, entrapped, or otherwise involved in some form of sinful activity. The point of clarification has to do with those who need to be addressed concerning these activities. It appears that the church in Corinth—as is the case in many contemporary churches (or Christians)—has taken to withdraw from, and at times ostracizing, those who are engaged in the activities that Paul lists here in the text. The problem, as Paul points out, is that to withdraw from those outside of the community of faith, who practice such activities, is to withdraw from life in general. The world has no such restrictions against the majority of these activities, at least to some degree. Sexual immorality and swindling may have legal restrictions, based on the moral and legal structures of a given community, but as for greed and idolatry, there may not be any restrictions over these.

Paul is clear in the text that this is referring directly to those who are within the community of faith that is indulging in these activities. Paul will go on at the end of this text to explain that it is God who will judge those who are outside the community of faith. As members of this community, it is our obligation to hold those within the community to a much higher standard. It should also be noted that the very warning in the text also makes it clear that those within the church are not to join the non-churched in indulging in the activities described here. According to the text, those who refuse correction and restoration, are to be put out of the assembly, that they might fall under the judgment of God.

The discussion concerning the extent of the exclusion of the erring brother/sister looks into the phrase, "Do not even eat with such people." The point of contention is centered around the intended meaning of this phrase "not even eat." The term itself is rather generic in that it could very well refer to any form of social gathering. Friberg identifies this term as having a social association together, thus resulting in a social isolation of the individual.[26] This is a position that is supported by Lange, that this text was to restrict the "intimate companionship" that would be present in sharing a meal socially with a fellow member of the church. While Jameson, Faust, and Brown share this position they further extend it to be applied to the Lord's Table as well. While there does seem to be some logic to the exclusion from the social setting, it would seem that a reading that places this in the context of Holy Communion should be favored. The church is

---

26. Friberg et al., *Analytical Lexicon of the Greek*, 366.

not commanded to abandon those struggling in sin, but to treat them as those who need to be won to Christ again (Matt 18:17).

Yet the wording seems to support the broader application which includes the social isolation of the unrepentant brother or sister, not just the Lord's Table. However, it should be noted that this passage follows the addressing of a situation where an individual who was part of the community of faith was flagrantly flaunting their sin. Paul has clarified that the church is not to avoid such contact with those in the world who practice such sinful activity, only those who are members of the community of faith. This raises the question if this distinction could be the identification of those within the community of faith, possibly suggesting the exclusion at the Lord's Table rather than the broader application? Fee acknowledges that this is not an issue that can be easily resolved. However, the context seems to lean towards the inclusion at the Lord's Table, as Paul has already addressed the issue of social exclusion when he instructed the church not to associate with those indulging in sinful practices. The instruction for social exclusion here, twice stated, is first directed almost exclusively toward the sexually immoral brother, then restated with a more inclusive application. Following the second instruction, Paul adds the phrase in question, not to even eat with such a person. Unless Paul is anticipating a situation such as sharing a table at a food court in a mall, then the flow of this discussion appears to have problems. The first of the two exclusionary instructions certainly are directed at social interaction, with the third—if we accept it as a directive concerning social interaction—being directed towards the Lord's Table. Apart from this, it would seem to be suggesting that Paul is expecting the Corinthian church to ignore his previous instructions. The expelling of the wicked person is in line with the treatment of them as an outsider, a pagan or tax collector, someone outside the community. While a pagan and tax collector would be welcome to come and listen, to learn and hopefully respond to gospel, they would remain outsiders until such a time as they responded to grace.

Old Testament Patterns

In the New Testament there is a distinct and unique nature in the approach to disciplining those who claim to be part of the community of faith, the application of grace. That is, it depends largely upon the extent of public knowledge and involvement. The patterns set down in these selected passages are instructions to the church and the practice isn't unique to the people of God, however, in the Old Testament, banishment/death was at times more the rule than the exception (Josh 7:20–27). What is unique is that these instructions are now also given to the church to enact. This type of discipline is practiced throughout the Old Testament, but in the New Testament the opportunity to repent and be restored is the rule not the exception. While the following examples are not intended to be exhaustive, it will provide insight into the character of our God and his dealings with sinful man, namely that sin has the ability to alienate us from God.

We can start at the beginning—that is, the creation narrative and the explanation concerning the fall of man. The first sin, that which took place in the garden of Eden, is an excellent example of all sin. Consider then, that we have two very different types of sin, the first being unintentional sin, and the second, willful sin.

> There is a strange twist in this episode that needs to be noted. This is that the woman was tempted and deceived (3.1, 13). Adam however, intentionally disobeyed. This means that Adam (and not Eve) is the fountainhead of human sinfulness (Rom. 5.12). The principle here is that there is a difference between unintended, and inadvertent sin and willful sin.[27]

Thus sin, in both of its origins has the same outcome, spiritual death (disfellowship) and banishment from the garden of Eden (excommunication). These two actions, which are the disciplinary function of the narrative, are both repeated throughout the Old Testament. How do these then connect to the New Testament practice of church discipline?

Often it is the case that the church or the leadership of the church attempts to discern the motivation behind a sinful incident, situation, or practice. For Adam and Eve, they are clearly not removed from the fellowship of the saints; they are, however, removed from the direct fellowship with the God of the saints. They are not entirely alienated from each other. However, there is a rift that is now developed between themselves and the God they were to have fellowship with. This is by far a more impacting and devastating action. The outlined situation here in Genesis is a foreshadowing of the discipline that Paul requires in 1 Cor 5:2. There are a few notable similarities. First, the sin at the center of the various narratives is hardly questionable. The first incident is in direct opposition to the instructions of God, the latter is a form of sexual perversion. Also, these sins are public, at

---

27. Stronstad, *Pentecostal Biblical Theology*, 15.

this point in history there was no hiding this sin from anyone, Adam and Eve may have tried (Gen 3:8–13) but their sin was found out (Num 32:23), literally everyone knew about.

The pattern of banishment/exile is a repeatable pattern throughout the Old Testament. This is the methodology that God uses to correct and discipline his people in both portions of the divided kingdom of Israel and Judah. To be removed from, first, the very presence of God, and then the presence of his people, the community of faith where people could once again encounter the reality of the living God, was indeed the crux of punitive action. However, for those who were willing to repent, the punitive action becomes corrective, as those under the penalty of exile were welcomed back, and then the center of their worship was restored. Therefore, the rebuilding of the temple which is recorded in the book of Ezra could very well be a foreshadowing of the restorative efforts that were to be brought to bear in the life of a repentant believer.

The purpose of looking back into the Old Testament is not an attempt to justify the corrective/restorative activity which is directed by God in the New Testament. Rather, the purpose is to briefly illustrate that this activity, in trying to reclaim the lives of those who are either being tempted to play with sin or already struggling within sin's grasp, is not a new idea within God's activity with his people. The community of faith, throughout the ages, has had its struggles regarding remaining faithful in its relationship with God and the encroaching sin in the lives of its members.

There are two essential points we need to take away from this. First, the disciplinary structure is built around the turning and restoring of a person back to their place within the community of faith and fellowship with God. Second, that there is a way to deal with and correct the sin as part of the process, but the rescue of the soul remains the priority. This is in keeping with the declared purpose of Christ himself, "On hearing this, Jesus said to them, "It is not the healthy who need a doctor, but the sick. I have not come to call the righteous, but sinners" (Mark 2:17; cf. Matt 9:12; Luke 5:31). Regathering those who belong to Christ and yet stray should be the priority of the church. In his high priestly prayer, Jesus prayed that he had not lost one that the Father had given him. Therefore, as the body of Christ, we must be about the business of our Lord, that is to seek and save those who are lost, including those who have strayed from the fellowship with God.

Having established the biblical format in dealing with sin, it must now be brought forward to the current standing of the church in the modern day. Much of the structure remains but with the application within the context of the modern environment, it is highly unlikely that they dealt with lawyers in a similar fashion to that of our current reality. Keeping this in mind, it becomes essential to clearly define our approach to those involved in sinful activity in the church as well as the biblical basis upon which this approach is based. Hence, continuing in the next chapter is how this paradigm might be applied in such a way as to protect the assembly from possible legal repercussions. Following this, an examination of the various sins that are specifically listed will be undertaken for the purpose of beginning to lay the groundwork for an adaptive restoration for the church.

Chapter Three _____

The Balancing Act

THE PROCESS OF CHURCH discipline is somewhat like walking a tightrope: lean a little too much to one side or the other and the results are disastrous. If there is no forward movement, and the precarious position is maintained, disaster is inevitable. The same type of tragedy will result if the church acts too aggressively in the approach to discipline and it merely becomes a punitive action. How then is progress to be made in this vital yet volatile ministry in the church? It would seem crystal clear to follow the procedure laid down in Scripture, yet there are issues that the church deals with today that the early church did not—lawsuits, legal entanglements, even varied denominational positions that may or may not reflect an accurate picture of what true holiness is. Careful and prayerful application of the text to any situation requires wisdom and patience. With the leading of the Holy Spirit it is very likely to see the saint restored.

  For a church to act upon on an accusation, there should first be a number of items in place. Primarily, the accusation should come from a reliable source. The best-case scenario in the definition of a reliable source would be a regular member of the church in good standing. There has been debate concerning what membership in the church entails, what distinguishes members from attendees in any given assembly. Membership in the body of Christ, the community of faith, is through the acceptance of the lordship of Christ. That is by having some form of salvific experience, a coming to faith regardless of the format, which could be some form of a crisis event. An individual may also come to a place of faith by way of gradual growth spiritually, where they take tiny steps of faith towards God and then have a "conversion" experience at some point. Either way, both end up in a dynamic relationship with Christ and are thus members of the body of Christ.

Church membership is not entirely separate from membership in the body of Christ, but neither are the two identical. One may be a member of one group and not be a part of the other; however, to grow as a member of the body of Christ, one must be part of a local body.[1] Throughout the New Testament there are numerous passages that speak edification of the saints through the church and that they can experience the power of Christ through the unity of the body. (1 Cor 1:10; 5:4; 14:26; Eph 2:21, 22; 4:16; Col 2:2) Furthering this point there is a prohibition of the neglecting gathering together; this gathering is the church (Heb 10:25). An example of an outline of the church disciplinary process may be viewed in appendix A, a portion taken from the "Local Church Constitution" of the Pentecostal Assemblies of Canada.

The point comes back to what designates membership within the local church and how does one obtain it? This is frustrated by the way some in the community of faith look for or choose a church, "In a consumer society, consumers are more committed to getting their needs met than they are to a community of people."[2] Thus, we have many in the church that are less likely to submit to the authority of the leadership of a church. Mark Lauterbach clarifies what the church should be: "it is a community of those who abandon themselves for the purpose of Christ."[3] "Though a bit more speculative, it may be possible to go further and say that we are identified as a member of the body of Christ in the universal sense through Spirit baptism, and we are identified as a member of a local body of Christ through water baptism (see Acts 2:41)."[4] The first sense is invisible, and the latter has to do to with the visual, public identification with Christ. The problem arises in the issue of submission to authority, such as the authority of the church.

Complaint

False accusations can destroy lives, marriages, and future ministries. As mentioned above, a complaint should be delivered by a member in good standing—not that a complaint by a non-member should be discarded. The

---

1. This is where some less than positive teaching has crept into the church, that an individual may be a Christian without belonging to a church.
2. Hammett and Merkle, *Those Who Must Give an Account*, 8.
3. Lauterbach, *The Transforming Community*, 48.
4. Hammett and Merkle, *Those Who Must Give an Account*, 18.

church, including its leadership, is not omniscient. They serve an omniscient God, but they themselves are not. In the previous chapter, the text from Matt 18 concerning who should initiate a disciplinary process was examined. The conclusion from the text was that there are no restrictions as to who should begin the disciplinary process. Therefore, dealing with sin in the initial stages is open to those who are "spiritual"/mature in the faith (Gal 6:1). Therefore, it is probably the safest to leave this in the hands of those in leadership, or at the very least to consult with those in leadership.

A complaint should be delivered, if at all possible, in writing, to assure that the subject of the complaint is a conveyance of verifiable, factual information. There does not need to be much detail, just a letter outlining the concerns of one member regarding the beliefs or conduct of another member. As for what requires the full attention of those in the leadership of the church, the sins that need correction, this will be explored in the next chapter. How this needs to be handled today is what will be discussed throughout this chapter. Once a complaint, concern, or burden has been brought to the those in leadership, several things should happen. First, the complaint should be evaluated for its validity, as concerns may be brought to those in leadership which may turn out to be non-sin related, but still, need to be addressed. Secondly, if there is some validity to the complaint, that is more than just a rumor, then it needs to be investigated, to determine what exactly needs to be done. Should there be even a hint of a child's involvement, legal professionals must be consulted without any delay. There may be other situations where, ethically authorities should be consulted. However, in most if not all jurisdictions any situation where a minor is involved must be reported to the appropriate authorities. Thirdly, it would be prudent to investigate the matter somewhat before the initial confrontation, or meeting.

Now, there are very few in leadership positions in the church that have the type of training to conduct a police-style investigation. It would hardly be a positive addition to any church to have a policed atmosphere. However, having someone who can ask the right type of questions and get to the heart of the matter more swiftly, is beneficial. Turning a long, drawn out process and streamlining it into a well-focused investigation can assist in determining guilt or innocence quickly and quietly with less fallout. Pastors are trained researchers, who have been taught how to analyze according to context. This usually means sitting down with the text of Scripture and asking the right questions, beginning with the basics. Who is named in the text, what are they doing and why, and then moving on to deeper questions concerning the text. To investigate a matter that could require church discipline is simply sitting down and asking the right questions once again of broken, sinful people who may be limping through life bearing the painful injury of sin. The church is to be like Christ to those who have stumbled, "a bruised reed He will not break" (Isa 42:3). To this end, going into this process with as much knowledge as possible is vitally important.

Questions

After a complaint is received, it must be investigated. In the contemporary church, it is necessary to examine the situation prior to undertaking any formal disciplinary action. What then might be considered as formal disciplinary action and what is informal? Jay Adams offers his definition of these two terms beginning with the diagram below.

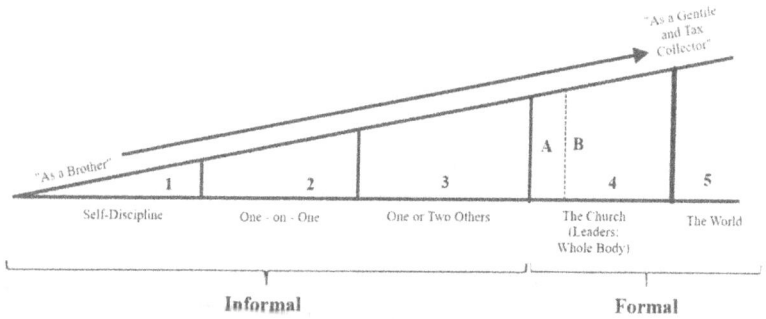

Figure 1: Adam's Diagram[5]

What Adams defines as "informal" extends from the sinful act through to the challenge by two or more brethren. However, as soon as the sin is known by anyone in the community of faith, that is, it has gone beyond an issue of self-discipline, it is now part of the formal instruction of the Savior and is now "formal" discipline. It might be a better classification to start with "Personal" discipline, that is the first stage, then "Private" discipline, stages 2 and 3, then finally "Public" discipline stages 4 and 5.

---

5. Adams, *Handbook of Church Discipline*, 27.

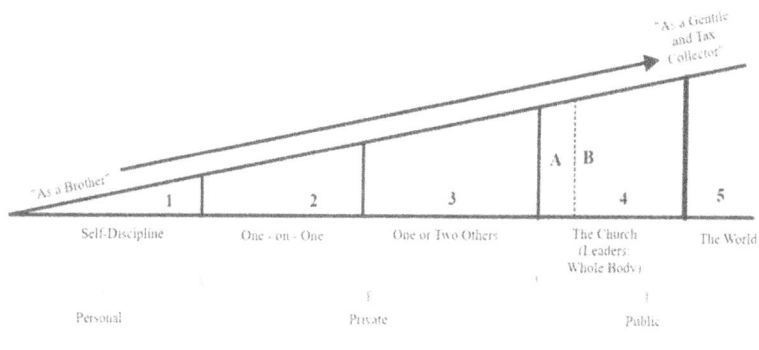

Figure 2: Adjusted Diagram

In asking the right questions, it is very probable that in the approach to dealing with the situation of sin in the life of the believer, the person's conscience could be pricked causing them to repent and ask for help.

Asking questions should be part of every level of the disciplinary process, as it will help in defining the scope of the process. Consider a hypothetical report that one member of a church was seen entering a hotel with a member of the opposite sex. While the question, "You were seen last Wednesday going into the hotel with a member of the opposite sex, can you explain?" seems to cover the issue, the wording has details that may not need to be conveyed to the individual involved. What if this is not merely a one-time occurrence with a member of the opposite sex? A better wording of the question would be, "Can you provide any insight into why you were seen going into a hotel with a member of the opposite sex?" Granted, this is not a great rephrasing of the question, but it does leave three areas open-ended: the "when," the "where," and the "who." A one-time occurrence will be easy to determine, as the details will be provided by the individual involved—unless the individual involved is very well-versed in providing false information. Rather than giving up information, a person who is involved in repeated offenses will have questions concerning the details themselves.

The process must not be confined to the accused (for a lack of a better term). All involved in the situation should be interviewed, to glean all information pertaining to the problem at hand. Granted, this must stay within the circle of those already confirmed to have knowledge of the incident(s). Being watchful of the attitudes of the accused (repentance or resistance), will be the key factors in determining the attitude of the heart. If there is honest, sincere repentance, then the process of discipline has been resolved and the process of restoration becomes active. But before restoration can begin, unless there is an immediate repentance, then certain saints will need to be confronted with their sin.

The First Approach

Between the Two of You (Private)

Once the charge against a member of the community of faith is established, the action must begin with some form of addressing the issue at hand, that is, to confront the person. Not everyone is comfortable in confrontation. It is a skill that some are sorely lacking. Many in the position of being disciplined by the church will object, attempting to cite the grace of God as a defense against the disciplinary action. Here it is important to take note, "Grace disciplines,"[6] grace does not leave a saint in their sin, grace challenges, calls out to redemption, first through the Spirit, then through the church. To continue in the grace of God is to submit one to another, being disciplined in love and growing beyond the confines of our personal struggle against sin. Once the process has moved beyond the confines of the person dealing with sin, it is now time that formal disciplinary procedures are put into play.

The process that Christ has provided from Matt 18:15–17 begins with a very narrow scope, a one-on-one approach. Adams recognizes this aspect and comments on the passage. "The principle followed in Matthew 18:15ff is that a matter must be kept as narrow as the event itself."[7] There is hardly anything informal about it. However, it must be handled at every level with the same grace that will forgive and rinse away the sinful stain. Sin is a serious matter and must be met with the full resources of the community of faith which are founded in the rich grace of God. At the same time, we need to be careful because we are dealing with the sin-damaged hearts of the family. This is a double-sided coin, as we must be gentle in dealing with the injured, yet at the same time remember that an injured person will wince and withdraw from the pain accompanying the healing hands of a doctor, as will a sin-inflicted saint from the care of a brother.

---

6. Lauterbach, *The Transforming Community*, 58.
7. Adams, *Handbook of Church Discipline*, 45.

The way the church has often responded to both those outside the covenant community and those inside who act like those outside has had an overly negative effect on both. "Clearly the tone of the reproof should be redemptive so that the one who is reproving pleads urgently for the repentance of the one who committed the offense."[8] From the start, the first interaction with the one who has become entangled with sin needs to be grace. It must be the principle that guides all the activities within the disciplinary process.

Confrontation often ends very badly, and nobody involved wants to be part of it regardless of whether they are doing the confronting or being confronted. Preparing to confront a person is essential and needs to begin with prayer, and each confrontation to follow can build on the efforts of this encounter. Then one needs to consider all of their own thoughts and emotions concerning the specific situation at hand. Being careful not to allow a person's own issues to cloud the situation is vitally important. As Laney writes,

> As I initiate a personal confrontation of this nature, I first remind myself of how I have failed in the past even as this brother or sister has. I think of how I was corrected or how I would want to be treated if I slipped into such a situation again. . . . Then before the confrontation takes place, I bring the matter before the Lord in prayer.[9]

What everyone in leadership who is involved in the process of church discipline needs to remember is that everyone is broken and tainted with sin. Not one is perfect, each one brings their own brokenness into this process. "What do you call a group of sinful Christians with different personalities, family backgrounds, life experiences, passions and preferences and who are also at different points in their growth in maturity and wisdom? The church!"[10] Forgetting that the church is the covenant community, the people of God, broken yet loved, adds an unstable element to the situation that can only be resolved through the cross. Those involved need to be examples of God's grace in relation to sin and repentance. This could very well take the form of approaching an erring member and beginning by seeking their forgiveness or testifying to the goodness of God that the leader has

---

8. Hammett and Merkle, *Those Who Must Give an Account*, 107.
9. Laney, *A Guide to Church Discipline*, 50.
10. Cheong, *God Redeeming His Bride*, 91.

experienced. As agents of grace, those involved in church discipline are like a field medic in a combat zone.

In sitting down with the patient, the medic needs to determine if the patient will live. This is called triage, the first step in providing aid to the injured. Part of this is established in the asking of questions. Some of these questions should answer the question concerning the mechanism of injury. mechanism of injury (MoI) explains how the injury happened. In a workplace injury on a construction site, the MoI might be a loose beam that fell and struck the worker. The first responder then learns of the beam strike and can begin to evaluate the possible injuries and how best to treat them. In dealing with a saint that has stumbled, the MoI is the sin that has overcome a brother or sister in Christ. An analysis of the various sins listed in the Scriptures, specifically those which require disciplinary action, will be reviewed in the following chapter. The earlier that the details of the offense can be verified, the easier the confrontation and the restoration will be. Provided that the offended saint responds and repents with the first encounter, the disciplinary action ends at this point and the restoration begins.

If the saint does not respond to the convicting power of the Holy Spirit, at the personal level of the disciplinary engagement, a leader will meet with the sinning saint. Church discipline is not engaged for God, it is engaged by God, and needs to be done according to his wisdom and grace. Grace, not man's view of justice, needs to the be bottom line. The church, the world needs agents of grace. "Earnestly, tenderly, Jesus is calling, Calling, O sinner, come home!"[11] Therefore those confronting should really be designated as agents of grace: "We are therefore Christ's ambassadors, as though God were making his appeal through us. We implore you on Christ's behalf: Be reconciled to God" (2 Cor 5:20). Regardless of saint or sinner, those who are caught in the snare of sin need to be beckoned home.

As for the actual physical meeting, this needs to be set up in a private space. The approach at this point should be more of a discussion than a confrontation. Inquiring rather than telling, even if many of the facts have been established and are confirmed. An inquisitive approach is far less threatening, the intent being not to put the erring saint on the defensive but to encourage him towards repentance—maintaining a non-confrontational atmosphere as the process allows the individual who has been caught in error the opportunity to repent in a place of grace and safety. The person involved here is a sheep that has strayed from the flock. The mission that

---

11. Thompson, "Softly and Tenderly," chorus line 2.

has been assigned by the Chief Shepherd is to care for the flock (Luke 15:4; Matt 10:6). Those involved in any form of disciplinary action should pray for a swift response of confession and repentance so that a plan to restore those who have stumbled can be implemented. Developing plans to restore the fallen will be discussed in the last few chapters. In all reality, those in leadership must be prepared to meet with denial and resistance and must, therefore, anticipate moving on the next step which is to meet again with the struggling saint, this time with two or three witnesses.

The Second Approach

One or Two Witnesses (Private)

It would be nice if everyone acted and reacted the way each of us as Christians should; however, this is not the reality that existed then or does today. It is at this level that many people's futures will be decided. Cheong has noted that "More often, people will often teeter back and forth between repentance and resistance, faith and fear, submission and rebellion."[12] As people are caught in this tug-of-war between the Spirit and those desires that are at war with the Spirit, they may need time to make the right choices. As such, there is no timeframe listed, and no issue with taking things slowly. Each situation must be dealt with according to its own merits. This is not a situational ethic; it is a flexible application of a fixed ethic, determined by those involved in the process.

Jay Adams makes a valuable point: "you must distinguish carefully between unwillingness to listen and a failure to understand or to accept your viewpoint on the matter."[13] A failure to understand is a significant issue. First, have those in leadership truly grasped everything that is going on in each situation? Granted, a matter of adultery shouldn't need much clarification, however, if the facts concerning an affair are in question, the confronted may have reasoned themselves out of the situation. Those who love God will stumble and, from time to time, may sear their consciences with a hot iron (1 Tim 4:2) so that they may have placed a blind spot over their sin. It may take time and creativity to determine the appropriate method of exposing their own sin to themselves.

---

12. Cheong, *God Redeeming His Bride*, 119.
13. Adams, *Handbook of Church Discipline*, 58.

Jesus' instruction to "take one or two others along" for the purpose of establishing the matter is most likely in keeping with the Old Testament instruction from Deut 17:6, 19:15, and Num 35:30, which require more than one witness for the conviction of a crime. There is some discrepancy concerning who would qualify as a witness. Laney puts forward the idea that a witness must be an actual witness in some sense to the sin which is at the heart of the disciplinary process. While those called up as witnesses may not have previous knowledge of the event, Laney argues that the qualification stands under the following condition: "Even if he has never seen such behavior, if the sinner during the confrontation admits his act, the witness has become a bearer of evidence."[14] While the reasoning can be followed, this really doesn't place the witness in this context as a "bearer of the evidence" of the original offense, all it really does is place the witness as a bearer of what transpired at the meeting where this evidence was discussed.

So then, the purpose of the witness is to assure that the discipline that takes place is both fair and impartial and that the accused has a clear understanding of all that is happening. Consider the issue of adultery, which was mentioned above. There may be a number of scenarios that could appear to be strongly suggestive of an adulterous relationship, and yet be completely innocent. The presence of witnesses could very well act as a check and balance to assure that both parties are being clearly understood by each other. An issue concerning discipline may be pursued that doesn't meet the criteria for what could be defined as a serious sin. Leeman attempts to explain what serious sin must look like: "Formal church discipline should occur with sins that are outward, serious and unrepentant."[15] The two points, both preceding and following the designation of "serious" would play a part in the definition of what a "serious" sin might be; however, it is not enough. It is highly probable that it isn't the sin that should be regarded as being serious enough but the attitude of the sinner. This would be directly connected to the "outward" and "unrepentant" qualifiers.

Even while dealing with the hardest unrepentant hearts, discipline must be conducted with grace. What may appear to be a person responding in satanic arrogance in resisting a seemingly appropriate call to repentance may simply be the struggle to find their way through a situation that has come crashing down on them. "The refusal must be a genuine one. This

14. Laney, *A Guide to Church Discipline*, 53.
15. Leeman, *Church Membership*, 54.

means that if in the heat of battle, he will not listen to reason, you will wait until he has had time to cool off and then try again."[16] This is one of the areas where the witnesses may be valuable in the ongoing discussions, that is, to recognize when the situation is getting too tense when emotions are flared and hot and it needs to come to a halt while the parties involved cool down and take stock of all that has transpired. It is important to keep in mind at this point that "biblical discipline is not vindictive but restorative"[17] (Matt 18:15; Gal 6:1; Jas 5:19–20).

Therefore, this is not a meeting that should be rushed, or for that matter confined to simply one session. Rather, it should be viewed as a process. What the text clearly lays out as the primary, or highest purpose is the restoration of one caught in sin (Gal 6:1). One of the key points in the text is the adjective "gentle," which qualifies "how" the restoration should take place. Restoration is the primary target of the process, especially at this point. After this step, the entire procedure is no longer in any way private but moves into the public stage. Repentance at this point is certainly desired and worked towards. Should the offending saint repent, then the disciplinary process comes to a halt and the restorative process begins. However, if repentance is not forthcoming at this point, then those involved are to take it to the church.

The Third Approach

Take it to the church (Public)

This is the penultimate stage in the church disciplinary process. There may be some that see this as the final stage, but it is not. While that isn't really the point of taking the issue to the church, it is still part of the process. Cheong notes concerning the condition of the heart: "The chronic heart condition will take one of three broad trajectories when it is exposed: (1) godly sorrow leading to repentance, (2) worldly sorrow leading to despair, and (3) little to no sorrow leading to all-out rebellion."[18] The first condition that Cheong notes is of course the preferred to see in the life of an erring saint, as this will most likely lead to both confession and repentance, hopefully before the disciplinary action has reached this point. The second

16. Adams, *Handbook of Church Discipline*, 57.
17. Hammett and Merkle, *Those Who Must Give an Account*, 118.
18. Cheong, *God Redeeming His Bride*, 120.

condition will at the very least begin to move the saint in the generally correct direction that God can turn into brokenness, which may then lead to repentance. It is the final rebellious position that presents the problem; the refusal to acknowledge the sin that so easily entangles. All it takes is for temptation to present itself at the correct opportunity for a saint to be compromised. Mark Lauterbach comments on this by stating, "The church is made up of saints who are not yet perfect."[19] He goes on to discuss the issue of indwelling sin, which is a part of the human condition, and as such, sin will plague everyone on this side of eternity.

Bringing them before the congregation is not meant to be a humiliating act, rather it brings the full arsenal of God to bear on the sin which is festering in the life of the believer, the purpose of which is to expel the sin and bring health back to the body—in the same way that a doctor in cleaning a wound will apply a topical antiseptic to the injury. If it appears that infection is setting in, a more aggressive approach may be taken, cleaning the wound more thoroughly, flushing it with saline and finally prescribing antibiotics which will be introduced into the whole body to kill the infection that the tissue might be saved. Hopefully, the parallel drawn in dealing with sin in the life of the believer/church is apparent.

As the matter is taken to the church there may well be mixed emotions and reactions. How could the church treat a beloved child of God so heartlessly? But there is nothing heartless in following the instructions of Christ. In fact, this is the most loving way of dealing with the issue. Standing around after an accident while a victim bleeds to death is no kindness; rather the spiritual first aiders need to rush to the scene, apply pressure to the wound, stabilize the patient, and get the patient to the hospital for further treatment. But really, is it truly a loving act to send them to what could seem to be a cold, impersonal hospital? YES! It can feel cold and impersonal, yet this is where the triage happens, and, hopefully, lives are saved.

Bringing the full arsenal of God to bear against the sin that is festering in the life of the believer takes shape in the many knees bent and heads bowed in prayer for their loved family member. The various people who will have spoken into this life will again provide words to encourage correction and repentance. The mighty army of God can rally around the wounded for support and protection. The reason it must be clear for bringing it to the church is that it's the final rallying of the Lord's earthly resources, his community of saints to come to the aid of those who need it the most.

---

19. Lauterbach, *The Transforming Community*, 130.

Dealing with People

Having established what needs to be done and why, the discussion now turns toward how to accomplish this. Concerning the instruction in Matt 18, the process of taking it to the church is hardly clear. "Obviously, these brief words lack a clear statement about how to carry out Jesus' instructions; no process for telling the church is even outlined, let alone detailed."[20] Adams is quick to recognize the difference between those within the covenant community and those who are in the congregation who are not yet believers. It would be pertinent to call together those who make up the covenant community from within the congregation in dealing with this matter. Bargerhuff comments, "Once the church has been made aware of the situation and the facts by the leadership, they in turn now have the opportunity to reach out to the unrepentant in an attempt to urge him or her to repentance."[21] In his discussion, Bargerhuff addresses the fact that in doing so churches often rush through part of the process and move immediately to the expulsion of the saint, thus meeting the conditions of "telling it to the church." In his discussion he disagrees with this position, saying, instead, this is an opportunity for the entire community to participate in the accountability for this soul. It is very possible that Christ intentionally left it this way for each community to work out for themselves how they might come to the aid of the sinfully disabled within the body.

Then, after a period—which should be spelled out at the very beginning of this part of the process, thereby giving the church an idea as to when to expect a final accounting of the individual's status—the church should be given a brief accounting of the process that has brought the issue to the point where it is brought before the church. It is also in this way the church can exhaust every option in reaching out to this member in every attempt to encourage them to repent and seek forgiveness and restoration. If at this point the individual involved repents, even as it is brought before the church, the disciplinary process ends, and the restoration begins.

However, if at this point the individual refuses to hear the call to repentance and continues in their sin, then the church has no other option but to expel them from the body. This is the final step in church discipline, the point where they are released and treated as a sinner or a tax collector (Matt 18:17). Later, in this chapter, the discussion will move towards

---

20. Adams, *Handbook of Church Discipline*, 68.
21. Bargerhuff, *Love That Rescues*, 148.

dealing with expulsion. At this point, there are two other matters in dealing with the disciplinary process that needs to be discussed. The first deals with two issues that are not related except in the number of steps involved in implementing them and the final matter is in relation to dealing with sin that is already public and needing immediate attention.

Leaders and Divisive Persons

Not every situation that requires discipline will follow the entire paradigm that Christ laid out in Matt 18. There are some situations that will require a modified approach. For those in leadership and those fostering divisive attitudes and doctrine, the three-step approach is eliminated. For both situations, the interaction is narrowed down to two basic approaches. Because of the narrowed approach, both will be discussed here, yet there are very distinct differences in the approach to each. While the text in Matthew concerning the disciplinary process at the very least allows for the inclusion of laypersons, at this stage all engagements should be conducted by those in leadership positions in the church. This diagram, which has been adapted from the diagram that Adams presents, gives a basic idea concerning the two approaches.

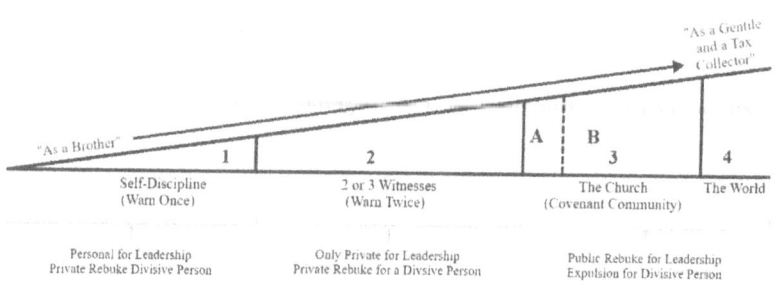

Figure 3: Adjusted for Leadership Application

Leadership

The first stage from Adams' diagram, which was renamed "the Personal Level" for the purposes of this discussion, is here still involving those in leadership, albeit at the personal level. God is at work in the heart bringing conviction and correction, dealing with the individual. When issues are dealt with at this level, and there is a sense of sincerity and integrity, it should be discussed at the board level. It may require a time off from ministry while the individual tends to his spirituality. Calling this, at this point, a formal restoration program may be unnecessary—even if sin has encroached, it has been dealt with. It would be advisable at this time to team the individual in leadership with an accountability partner to assure that steps are taken to restore the person's spiritual vitality.

Bringing any form of a charge against those in leadership is very different from bringing a charge against others in the church. To begin, the process starts not with a single individual bringing an issue to the leadership, rather Paul is crystal clear that this is something that needs to be done by two or three witnesses (1 Tim 5:17–25). In the text, Paul's instruction is that these "elders" should be reproved in front of everyone. First, the language suggests that the elders in question here are in a current, active commission of some form of sinful activity. Hammett discusses that even this must be brought before the assembly for full disclosure. "If an accusation of sin is verified then the elder guilty of the sin must be rebuked 'in the presence of all.'"[22] If the issue has been dealt with and the elder is in submission and repentance, then the appropriate course of action would be to acknowledge that the elder has been found in a situation of personal compromise. Therefore because he was in submission to others in leadership in the assembly and, that while he may be removed from his ministry position for a season—dependent on the outcome of the restoration program, he may resume his position of leadership. A great deal of the outcome would be dependent upon the elder's cooperation during the restoration process and all personal assessments that may be required of him/her.

What if the elder is not entirely cooperative with the disciplinary action that is taken against them? What if there is willful resistance and a clinging to the sin? Then reproving them before everyone would be the same as in the second-to-last stage of the disciplinary process that the laity

---

22. Hammett and Merkle, *Those Who Must Give an Account*, 127.

must go through. That is "taking it to the church." This would include the disclosure of the type of offense—although sharing details may not be entirely helpful. There is the possibility of this type of a meeting going well, and the elder standing up and making a confession (not in detail but the charge) and submitting to those who are currently in authority. Then as before, the disciplinary process comes to a halt and the matter shifts over into the restoration process. If, however, the elder remains entirely resistant throughout this stage, he must then be removed from the assembly, expulsion. "Leaders are not exempt from discipline, and they must not be treated with partiality."[23] This then will provide for a healthy fear of sin in the lives of the members of the church.

Divisive Members

Divisive members in the church have a different set of protocols for being dealt with. The reason being is the damage that they can do to the assembly. Paul's text to Titus appears clear: "warn them once." This warning is a word of admonishment and instruction, which is Paul's pattern for dealing with divisive people, those holding to and continuing to teach doctrines that are contrary to biblical doctrines. What Paul calls for is for those in leadership to provide corrective teaching, at the most twice, then if not heeded, to expel the member. There is no need expressed here for presentation to the body as the activity of expulsion will have already been determined by those in leadership, not on some arbitrary assessment, but by the individual's unwillingness to accept sound doctrine.

Full Public Knowledge

This group is separate from the rest in that there is no private admonishment whatsoever. That the sin is fully, publicly known dictates swift decisive action as is the case in 1 Cor 5:1–5. The sin listed here is one that is appalling still to this day, and it almost seems strange that Paul would have to address it. Paul's admonition to the church here is the swift removal of the individual. Bargerhuff cites Maria Pascuzzi stating, "The step-mother apparently was not a member of the church, or else Paul would have called for action against her

---

23. Hammett and Merkle, *Those Who Must Give an Account*, 129.

as well."[24] This makes sense as it would be hard for Paul to correct a double standard in the church by creating a second double standard. Therefore, the man in question was alone facing discipline.

However, this may not be an entirely negative thing; there are many who see the church as an institution that is corrupt. Numerous scandals which have taken place in the church have, to various extents, broken the public's trust. Dealing with situations like this openly, while showing some level of sensitivity, and cooperating with other authorities may very well reverse this loss of trust. A gentle but firm position needs to be taken, stating that while the beliefs of the church may be counter-cultural, as they have been in the past, that they will not change. While some activities may be acceptable and even considered moral in the public eye, they are not permitted within the community of the church. The challenge here will be to convey the message that these actions are meant not to be punitive but redemptive.

Expulsion

Handing over to Satan

Writing about times when expelling a member is necessary, Schreiner in the book, *Those Who Must Give Account*, has commented, "It is imperative to note that such situations are exceptional."[25] The expulsion of a member of the church is never an easy thing and it should never be considered as a normative activity in the church. To get to this level all other redemptive purposes must have failed. "Paul teaches us that excommunication is serious business."[26] This is a matter of gravest concern, and when a brother or sister refuses to listen to the council of either the Holy Spirit or the church, drastic measures must be undertaken to hopefully get his/her attention and turn their hearts back to God. "In either case, after the church leaders and congregation unsuccessfully have made every effort to bring the sinner to repentance, they must ostracize the offender from the church fellowship."[27] The point is to remove the individual from the com-

---

24. Bargerhuff, *Love That Rescues*, 160.
25. Hammett and Merkle, *Those Who Must Give an Account*, 105.
26. Jeschke, *Discipling the Brother*, 119.
27. Laney, *A Guide to Church Discipline*, 56.

munity, the actions of which will hopefully, finally draw the individual's attention to the gravity of the situation at hand.

Paul refers to this activity as turning the individual over to Satan (1 Cor 5:5; 1 Tim 1:20), the purpose of which is redemptive. In both cases, there is the message of hope combined with this drastic action, the first, concerning the incestuous individual in Corinth, "that his spirit might be saved." For the latter two, whom Paul mentions were blasphemers, teaching some aberrant doctrines, this may have been the process that Paul recommended to Titus, or, what Paul had mentioned in Titus was based on dealing with these two mentioned in his first letter to Timothy. Whatever the order, the point is these two were "turned over to Satan" to be "taught" not to blaspheme. What needs to be noted in both situations is that this activity was undertaken for the spiritual benefit of the individual involved. "The rebuke is designed to expose, convict, and convince the sinner of the need to repent."[28]

How this removal takes shape has been the subject of debate, whether this is to include an entire disassociation with the individual in question or to exclude him in some way from the community life of the assembly. From the various Scriptures that have been reviewed in this discussion, the bulk of the material would support community life exclusion. The reasons for this follow the bottom line in what both Jesus and Paul mention in their texts as needing to be considered as a redemptive component. For Christ those excluded should be treated as a pagan or tax collector, the very individuals that he came to seek and save (Luke 19:10). "This means that while making no *final* judgment about his actual heart condition, the church is to treat Him *as if* he were an unbeliever."[29] Paul had the persons that were teaching false doctrine put out of the assembly for redemptive purposes, in the case of the blasphemers to be taught not to blaspheme. In the case of the incestuous man, there is a clear pattern for his return that it seems Paul laid out in his second letter to the church in Corinth (2 Cor 2:5–11). It appears that this passage is directly connected to the incestuous man. The most significant single-person issue that is dealt with in 1 Corinthians is this very issue. Paul carefully instructs those in Corinth to forgive and comfort those that have responded to this last level of discipline.

The bottom line in all matters pertaining to the disciplinary ministry—yes, it is a ministry of the church—is that "the church is called to be a

---

28. Laney, *A Guide to Church Discipline*, 63.
29. Adams, *Handbook of Church Discipline*, 80, italics original.

redemptive community."³⁰ It is intended to be a medic station, with an active triage area to assist those who have been ravaged by sin. This includes those who are members of that community and have fallen beyond temptation into the very sin that they were freed from. The desire and target of church discipline, even at this level, is to see the individual turn from their wicked ways, confess their sin, and be restored to the body of Christ.

The following is an actual account that occurred many years ago.[31] A church was involved in various ministries including a street ministry in the city center. Many young people were encountering God and leaving the streets, many finding local churches that accepted, loved, and discipled them. A young lady had such an encounter with God and began to tentatively explore what it meant to grow in Christ. She was very hesitant; she had worked as a prostitute at times and was afraid of how those in the church would look at her. She began attending a church, and eventually caught the eye of a deacon's son. Those who knew of the interest that was developing between the two thought that this would be a positive relationship for the young lady. The young man found that the temptations of his passions were greater than he realized and the two were intimate together. How the couple was found out is unknown, but when asked about it, the young man boasted of his activity.

Shortly thereafter the disciplinary ministry of the church went into action and the young man was privately rebuked, first one-on-one, then when that failed, by two or three witnesses, one of which was a deacon in the church, his own father. He resisted the attempts of those calling him to repentance. Finally, the matter was brought before the church. He did not attend the meeting. The Scriptures relating to the situation were reviewed, and the church was informed that the young man was being "disfellowshiped" from the church. They were encouraged to pray for the young man. What happened to the young woman who had recently come to Christ? She disappeared, as the boasting of the young man left her humiliated.

Six months passed. People would see the deacon's son in passing on the street. They may or may not have acknowledged him; but no other efforts were made. He struggled with things at home, where he still lived with his family. Then, during an evening service as the pastor was teaching, he looked up from his notes, his eyes focused on someone in the back of the

---

30. Lauterbach, *The Transforming Community*, 124.

31. I was part of the team that formed the disciplinary advisory council that worked with the situation.

sanctuary, and he fell silent. A few moments passed, and he stepped back from the music stand that held his notes. The young deacon's son slowly approached the front of the church. As he stepped behind the music stand it was obvious that he was trying to catch his breath. He slowly looked up with tears in his eyes, confessed his sin, acknowledged that he had resisted all the efforts to correct him and call him to repentance. The complete nature of the sin was never disclosed, all that the church had been told was that it was a moral failure, one that required this level of intervention. The young man asked for forgiveness and to be restored to the fellowship of the church. The pastor never said a word. The entire congregation that was gathered that evening stood up, surrounded him, with many weeping as they welcomed home the lamb that the Savior had gone off to save.[32]

This event is evidence that, when properly conducted, church discipline works and works well. The young man's life was saved, and he committed to a closer walk with Christ. Tragically, the young lady was never heard from again.[33] This underscores the reality that sin destroys. To this end, sin must always be addressed, and the sinner disciplined. The saint must be challenged to forsake their sin, to seek godly counsel and to commit their way to the Lord. Anyone who has been involved in a situation where sin has encroached to the point where their fellowship with Christ and fellow believers has been compromised needs to be disciplined, corrected, then restored to the fellowship, and if possible, to any ministry areas that they may have been involved in. Shortly, the discussion will investigate how to develop a restoration program that will be the most effective in various situations and with different people. But prior to that, a look at what kind of sin requires discipline. The answer may seem to be easy, all sin. However, as mentioned previously, understanding the mechanism of injury greatly assists with the diagnosis and treatment of an injury, especially those of a spiritual nature.

---

32. The young man was welcomed back into the fellowship of believers. He willingly took part in the restorational process which was overseen by both the pastor and his father.

33. Throughout the process to minister to the young lady, she felt betrayed and crushed. A number of ladies reached out to her but with no success. While there are times when the efforts of the church may seem fruitless, they must be pursued for the sake of all involved. The Holy Spirit was not finished in the life of this young lady, nor was she forsaken.

Conclusion

Discipline is difficult. It is unpleasant and messy but vital for the life of the church. Yet moving through the various stages laid out in the text of Scripture provides the best possible method for challenging sin and calling a family member back to a deeper walk of faith. As the discussion has progressed through the various stages, with the help of various authors, saints have been challenged and given the opportunity to turn from sin. Looking at the patterns provided by Christ and his apostle, Pauline methodologies have been provided for this very purpose. The discussion has ventured through some issues that need to be considered in preparation for disciplinary confrontation.

The process of moving through the various stages of the disciplinary process as well as a few variant models have been reviewed. Correcting and calling the saint to repentance has been the preferred outcome at every step of the process. Even with what some may consider a saint's end, there is redemption and grace. The final chapters will discuss some of the issues that must be considered in developing a successful restoration model for specific situations. But before the conversation gets there, a discussion of the mechanism of injury is in order. What sin trapped this saint, what evil invaded the heart and so reduced their walk to a limp, to a crawl, and for some a dead stop?

Chapter Four _____

Defining the Problem

IN TALKING ABOUT THE church, the need and the process of discipline, the discussion has identified problems within the people of God, the community of faith. The "old man" that Paul alludes to is not quite dead yet, he rages on in our lives (Eph 4:22; Col 3:9). The reality of the lives of the redeemed is that each person lives fully in two realities. Each believer is *simul iustus et peccator*—a Latin phrase that means, "at the same time justified and sinner." The paradox of the life of faith is that we are torn between two worlds. Being the recipients of justification through the crucifixion, death, and resurrection of the Lord Jesus Christ, we are no longer under the curse of sin and yet the plague of sin still courses through our veins. Dr. Gordon Fee illustrates this tension with the motif "already/not yet." We are already partakers of the divine character through Christ Jesus, yet, as the apostle John so eloquently writes to the church, "If we claim to be without sin, we deceive ourselves and the truth is not in us" (1 John 1:8). Granted, John quickly spells out the remedy for the ever-present reality of sin in our lives: confession. What needs to be mentioned here is that John was writing to the church, to the community of faith. While he mentions confession, which is the acknowledgment of something, he is silent on repentance, which might be seen as the corrective response to confession.[1]

Although this is in no way intended to be an exhaustive study in hamartiology, there are some aspects of sin that need to be considered and understood. Unlike products for the home, sin does not come with a warning label, or for that matter a material safety data sheet.[2] Life would be

---

1. Various traditions may view this interaction differently. There may be a cause and effect relationship between the two. Regardless of how one may view it, from a theological standpoint the two are intrinsically linked.

2. The material safety data sheets (MSDS) are part of the designation from the

wonderful if sin came with an appropriate warning label. However, reality is very different. It is closer to cholate-covered arsenic. Sin needs to be seen for what it is, and what it does. There is a great deal of validity to the statement by Kenneth Klinghorn, "there is no precise biblical definition of sin. The Bible is concerned more with the remedy for sin than with a definition."[3] While there may not be a clear definition, having a better idea of the impact of sin will assist in repairing that damage. The truth of this weighs heavily on the heart as one tries to discover how beloved brothers and sisters in Christ are drawn away from the rich fellowship with our King and each other, into the muck and mire of sin that so easily entangles. "The story of the fall tells us that sin corrupts it puts asunder what God joined together and joins together what God had put asunder. Like some devastating twister, corruption both explodes and implodes creation, pushing it back toward the "formless void" from which it came."[4] The "void" reaches out and draws in those who think they are safe by knowing that it is there. But the problem lies in knowing it is there and yet being drawn to it. Paul states that by the very knowing of the law and what sin is, that people, including those in the community of faith, are drawn to it (Rom 7:8, 9).

When a person walks into the emergency room of almost any hospital the two questions that this person will face are: a) what is the problem and b) what happened? While these basic questions may very well be phrased differently, they cover what is at issue and how it came to pass in the person's life. As previously mentioned, in the first aid industry, the "mechanism of injury" is important to understanding the extent of the injury. Sin is an injury to the soul, albeit, all too often it is a self-inflicted injury, but an injury all the same. For instance, a person is brought into a trauma care center with serious burns. To treat the individual, it is vital to know whether they are chemical, thermal, or electrical burns, as all are treated differently, and the degree of the burn must also be taken into consideration. Using the wrong treatment can be disastrous. In the same way, if one were to use a one-restoration-plan-fits-all, it would be disastrous in restoring a compromised saint. This underscores the need to understand "why" something happened, as well as "how" something happened.

Canadian WHMIS (Work Hazardous Materials Information System), the Canadian equivalent of the Occupational Health and Safety Administration. The purpose of the MSDS system is to provide a quickly accessible resource concerning the hazards and first aid treatment to some of the various materials found in a specific work environment.

3. Carter et al., *A Contemporary Wesleyan Theology*, 237.
4. Plantinga, *Not the Way It's Supposed to Be*, 30.

Understanding how something happened does not negate the need to deal with it. The issue of sexual misconduct, for example, is one that demands discipline from the church. However, learning that the offender was a victim of some form of sexual abuse in the past would affect the restoration program—if the offender submits to the leadership in the church. The issue of a person who has been involved in swindling others out of their hard-earned money also needs to be addressed. But what impact would it have if, when investigating, it is learned that the offender has problems with a gambling addiction? That then also needs to be addressed in the restoration program, if it is in fact going to be addressed effectively. As the discussion moves through the various categories of sin, each will include an illustration which will clarify the interrelatedness in each area.

Within the New Testament, there are several sin lists that are provided for those sins which will most likely require some form of intervention. Because these lists are not identical, it is highly likely that these lists are not exhaustive. A brief analysis of some of these transgressions should provide a bit of an MoI to consider in discussing restoration programs.

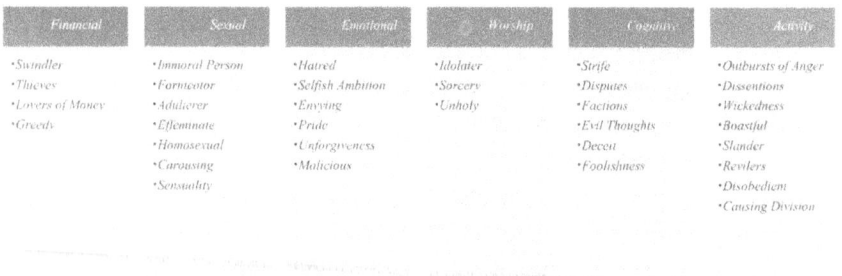

Figure 4: Categorization of Sin

Listed above are six basic areas that are listed within the pages of the New Testament (Mark 7:21–22; Rom 16:17; 1 Cor 5:11; 6:9, 10; Gal 5:19–21; 2 Tim 3:1–5; Titus 3:10). The following discussion will deal with an overview of each group, commenting on the specifics of some of the various transgressions. The purpose of this is to understand the nature of the offense to better assist those who are trying to free themselves from the hold of sin on their lives. Some of these transgressions may need far more correction than a simple rebuke. As stated previously, one of the initial pieces of information that an emergency first responder needs to know is the "mechanism of injury." How did the injury occur? This information is vital as it may alert the first responder to potential injuries that they would otherwise not know to look for. Some of the listed offenses may include a malicious attitude on the part of the offender, while others may suggest a person merely caught up in temptation. Still others may reflect a character deficiency that needs to be corrected. It would be wise to include in church documentation a statement restricting the disciplinary action of a church while a criminal case is being pursued.[5] Pursuing a church investigation could interfere with a possible criminal investigation and thus put the church in a precarious legal position. The purpose of church discipline is to restore a believer not to run interference with any possible criminal proceedings.

A) Financial

The matter of sins in relation to finances or the material holdings of any kind has four primary areas which are mentioned in Scripture. The first thing that is hopefully observed in the graphic is that each of the terms represents an aspect of sin in relation to an individual's or corporation's financial or material holdings. As well, there is an inter-relatedness to them while at the same time a distinctive nature to each. Considering that an individual may have some form of greed, this could be related to any number of items or issues. However, most often greed is associated with money and forms the basis for the love of money. The terms for both "greed" and "lovers of money" suggest that greed is a much stronger desire and compulsion for money. It may be suggested that there is an escalation in sinful activity as figure 5 illustrates. Each stage if left unchallenged feeds into the next exacerbating the problem. The lack of disciplinary intervention may result in this free fall into sins that have more serious natural consequences.

---

5. See appendix A, an excerpt from the Local Church Constitution of the Pentecostal Assemblies of Canada, bylaw 6, section 6.3.6. Regarding legal charges, subsection 6.3.6.1.1 reads as follows, "No disciplinary procedures will be followed until the legal proceedings, including appeal, have run their course."

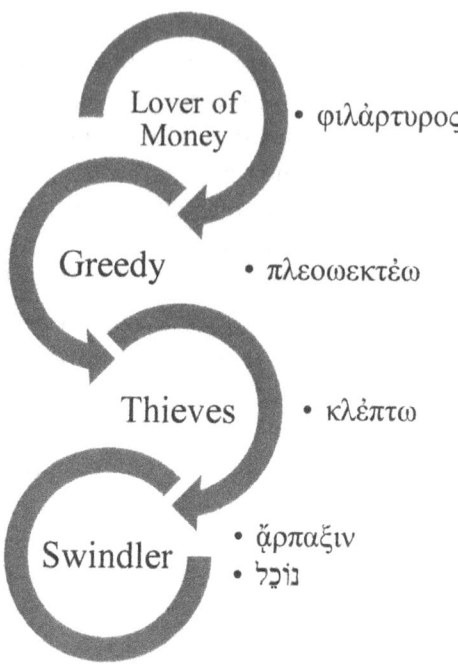

Figure 5: Escalation of Financial Sin

The author of Ecclesiastes declares that he who loves money never has enough (Eccl 5:10). This is in direct opposition to Paul's teaching to Timothy: "but godliness with contentment is great gain" (1 Tim 6:6). As the desire or love of money increases, greed takes hold and becomes a driving force in life. Greed is defined by the apostle Paul as a form of idolatry, which is among the things that a believer is to put out of their life (Col 3:5). This attitude, and the resulting conduct, is referred to as shameful. The general feeling that is depicted here is that God is no longer the goal of, or the fulfillment of, what the soul longs for, and that in the seeking of material possessions this fulfillment is perverted with the individual creating an idol for themselves.

Theft is a direct violation of the eighth commandment, "You shall not steal" (Exod 20:15; Deut 5:19). Theft may be a crime or sin of opportunity due to a perceived or real need, where what is accessible might be observed as the object of desire or need. There is along with this "need" and ease of access the sense that this may be acquired through stealth without the knowledge of any other. Along with theft, robbery may be included. While the two may be mistaken as referring to the same activity, robbery does have a different connotation. In the contemporary sense, robbery not only includes the acquiring of someone else's property illegally, but it includes violence or the threat of violence in the commission of the crime. When Christ speaks of the robbers in the parable of the Good Samaritan, the Greek term here is λῃστής, which carries the idea of violence in the commission of the offense (Luke 10:30). The term also applies to insurrectionists, that is, to those who are committed to overturning those in leadership which is usually accomplished through some form of violent action. The distinction is made of "one who seizes by violence," in contrast to "a thief one who uses stealth."

What may be the most corrupt form of financial sins is that of the swindler which not only has the idea of obtaining another's property by deception, but also with a sense of deliberate intention to do so. The basis of this charge can be found in the writings of the prophet Amos, who records the activity in this area as "trampling the needy" (Amos 8:4). Further is the use of dishonest scales to abuse those that require this service. God very clearly declares, "I will never forget anything they have done" (Amos 8:7c). While there is very little use of the term, from the Hebrew (נוֹכֵל) nokel (Mal 1:14) it basically means 'to be crafty, cunning and deceitful" or, Paul's use in the Greek (ἅρπαξιν) harpaxin (1 Cor 5:10) which adds to the definition a ravenous pursuit.

An interesting note concerning this text is that the activity seems to resemble the activity of Ananias and Sapphira in the New Testament (Acts 5:3, 4). The deceit here is the dedication of something to the Lord which is then not given. Vows, once made, were meant to be kept, especially those vows which were directed towards the Lord. The outcome of this action was to profane the name of the Lord, thus the deceit and dishonest actions and attitudes were secondary considerations. The basic structure strongly suggests a deeply dishonest and vehement approach to obtaining the possessions of another. The usage in both the Old and New Testaments deal with the dishonest representation of one's spiritual status and those involved in such activities.

There is the tension between thinking about these sins in strictly a profane or non-sacred way and the religious or sacred sense. "When we are thinking religiously, we view a shopkeeper's defrauding of a customer not merely as an instance of lawlessness but also of faithlessness, and we think of the fraud as faithless not only to the customer but also to God."[6] Swindling and theft are clearly criminal acts, outlined in various federal and regional/state criminal codes. Swindling is not recognized as a legal term. The definition under a legal system would be "fraud." Both issues, theft and swindling/fraud, have serious legal implications that will most definitely include the criminal legal system. Dealing with sins in this category, while they may be considered as financial, may include other forms of property. The basic considerations will be on how to deal with the sense of need and the possible compulsion to acquire what does not belong to them.

In dealing with the correction of those caught up in financial sin it would be wise to call upon one or more people with accounting skills. Those who become adept at the deceitful acquisition of material wealth often have advanced skills in hiding this "profit." Should a financial error be discovered in the church or higher levels of companies, a forensic accountant may be required—someone who has the confidence of the court—to analyze any and all materials pertaining to the error. Criminal charges are highly likely with sins in this area and any restoration attempts will have to wait until the criminal case runs its course. Some form of spending journal/spreadsheet to help the individual track and become aware of possible errant spending habits may prove helpful. In dealing with this and most areas of sin, some setbacks and slip-ups should be anticipated. Rather than allowing these to destroy the person entering the restoration phase, they should assist through these slip-ups.

---

6. Plantinga, *Not the Way It's Supposed to Be*, 12.

B) Sexual

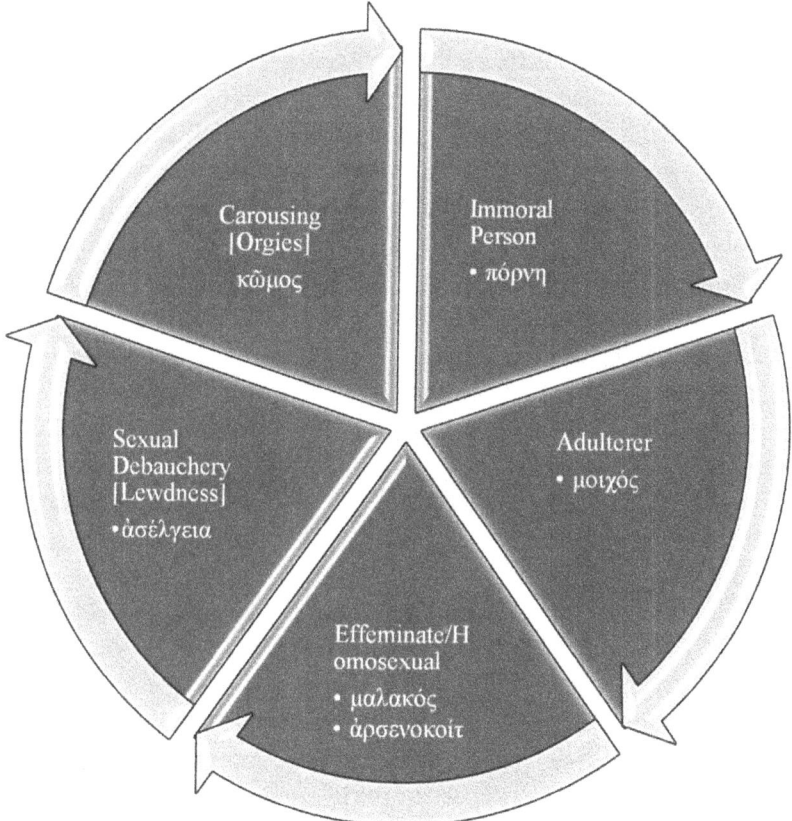

Figure 6: Interrelatedness of Sexual Sin

Sins of a sexual nature have a unique aspect to them; sexual sins are not only sins that have a sense of betraying God and oneself, but one's body as well (1 Cor 6:18). The entire area of sexually related sins is a difficult one as the damage caused is so much more far reaching, especially with some of the STDs that are currently in circulation. Figure 6 illustrates the cycle of sexual sin and lust, as one form is indulged lust for the next grows. As with all sin, shame is a debilitating factor. Yet the shame felt over various forms of sexual sin is increased due to public opinion. Especially for those in leadership, there is an added component and that is the power differential. In his book *Sex in the Forbidden Zone*, Dr. Peter Rutter discusses the impact that he felt when presented with a wounded woman approaching him sexually in his office. "Nothing in my training had prepared me for this moment. . . . I was overcome by an intoxicating mixture of timeless freedom, and the timeless danger, that men feel when a forbidden woman's sexuality becomes available to them."[7] Few are prepared for the struggle concerning this issue. Most ministerial training programs don't prepare the future ordinate for the intoxication of this power differential. Following that, few credentialed leaders are prepared to train those leaders under their care concerning this struggle. What is possibly the most frightening part about being in this type of situation is that the person in the power position does not recognize the influence that they have. "When a man has influence over both a woman's outer identity issues and her inner spiritual issues, the binding can be complete."[8] The power imbalance makes the resistance fade away and increases the sense of shame as there seems to be little else to be done in dealing with their sexual woundedness that Rutter suggests is a major part of the problem.[9] As the illicit sexual liaison fails to resolve the issue, the shame increases. In discussing Augustine's views, Henri Blocher comments, "He observes that the association of sin and sex, sex, and dirt, stems 'from deep-seated psychological factors'; he points to the enigmas built into our experience with sexuality and to the frightening power of sex, which 'can wreak untold sorrow in the form of shame, jealousy, rivalry, and violence.'"[10] Possibly one of the most insidious aspects of sexual sin for those who are caught up in it is the shame that is heaped upon them from both external and internal sources. The external from those both in the church and society, the internal as the individual tries to rebuild their "Christian" identity.

The immoral person is addressed in 1 Cor 5:11 and Gal 5:19. A serious moral compromise is more than simply an individual with poor sexual boundaries. There is the support that by utilizing this terminology Paul is pointing to a greater threat than an out-of-control sense of sexuality, that this includes a sexualized form of spirituality. He brings this to the attention of the church in Corinth where it is reported that there were over a thousand courtesans dedicated to Venus for cultic prostitution.[11] This sense

---

7. Rutter, *Sex in the Forbidden Zone*, 4.
8. Rutter, *Sex in the Forbidden Zone*, 34.
9. Rutter, *Sex in the Forbidden Zone*, 61, 65.
10. Blocher, *Original Sin*, 113.
11. In the contemporary world we may not see temples built for cult prostitution, but it was a practice in the days of Paul and earlier.

DEFINING THE PROBLEM

of sexuality, which has vast spiritual connotations, also has roots in ancient Babylon where a woman was required once in her lifetime to "'sacrifice' herself to the goddess Mylitta by giving her body to a stranger in the temple precincts."[12] While these may not be the practices which the contemporary church deals with, it does deal with issues such as "friends with benefits." It is a skewed view of sexuality. This extends to the contemporary use of pornography, which, according to Josh McDowell, is "probably the greatest threat to the church in its existence."[13] Whether or not McDowell is correct, or a person agrees with him, porn is a problem.

The sin of adultery has the denotation of the involvement in any form of sexual practice of a married person outside the confines of the marriage covenant. In the context of the New Testament, the sin of adultery was equally applied to both male and female, whereas in the Old Testament, and in classical Greek usage, the idea had a slightly more misogynistic tone to it. This was due to the concept that the woman held the keys to the integrity of the family or clan regarding the family line. Some of this view still exists in popular culture, where a sexually promiscuous man may be viewed as a "stud" but a woman as a "slut." Paul's application of the terminology does not have the same perspective to it. In Paul's view, the two are to be viewed as equal, either they are maintaining the vows of the covenant of marriage or they are not, regarding the monogamous sexual relationship. Much of this has as its foundation in the allegorical view that marriage reflects the relationship between God and his people, first Israel and currently, the church.

Homosexual practices have been soundly condemned throughout the Scriptures (Lev 18:22; 20:13; Rom 1:26–28; 1 Cor 6:9; 1 Tim 1:8–11). In the common practice of the day, in the surrounding cultures, the attitudes were varying concerning same-sex relations.[14] Paul confirms the New Testament position through the text in 1 Corinthians and in Rom 1. The very act is condemned and framed by Paul as the result of idolatrous attitudes in man, replacing the Creator with the creation as the object of worship. Paul clearly labels the activity as a perversion of God's natural order (Rom 1:26, 27).

This does little to clear the murky waters with the current views of many concerning gender identification. How does one deal with this sin in the light of many falling into areas such as gender neutrality, or gender fluidity? The

---

12. Brown, *New International Dictionary*, vol. 2, 497.
13. Merritt, "Pornography."
14. Encyclopædia Britannica, "Homosexuality."

issue of gender identity is currently a difficult area to deal with and may require more resources than many churches have available.

The primary aspect of this specific sin-group is that it leans very heavily on life according to the desires of the flesh, enjoying the sensual pleasures—the hedonistic lifestyle. It is because of these same sensuous desires that the younger widows were encouraged to get re-married lest they are drawn away from Christ (1 Cor 7:10–11). In this context, they may be seen as almost overwhelming desires that are continually building until eventually sweeping people off their feet.

Originally the term was applied to a feast in honor of a Greek deity, where there would be excessive eating and drinking. The core idea here is the complete lack of restraint in the pursuit of pleasure. While the level of sexual sin in the church may not extend to this extreme, the very use of some of the terminology used to describe sexual, sinful activity illustrates that the possibility is there. Whether it be the abuse of power by a member of the leadership in the church or adultery, homosexuality, or pornography, the possibility for sexual sin is present and dealing with it means understanding its draw and nature. Man is a sexual being, nothing will change that. Some have tried, yet sexual expression remains a part of life, both appropriate and inappropriate. The latter needs to be dealt with. The resulting shame may very well cripple the offender from responding effectively to those calling them back into a healthy relationship with God and his people.

Many books concerning discipline in the church deal with credentialed ministers and the issue of sexual sin. There is no argument that this poses a unique and entirely debilitating situation for both the minister and the church. The larger problem is that this type of sin is hardly restricted to those in leadership. In dealing with an individual who has ventured into the area of sexual sin, there are several considerations that will assist in the restoration. Throughout the process close support and accountability is imperative. The Promise Keepers men's movement would regularly encourage men to challenge each other concerning what they were putting before their eyes. Promises 3 and 4 of the Promise Keepers movement are centered on this very issue. Promise 3 includes avoiding sexual impurity, promise 4 to build strong marriages.[15] Another point here is to assist in the establishing of healthy personal boundaries. In any illicit sexual engagement, boundaries are extremely blurred. For restoration to take place healthy boundaries need to be established. This may be complicated if there were no healthy boundaries in place

---

15. Promise Keepers, "7 Promises," promise 4.

to begin with. Assisting the individual to locate safe places while they are rebuilding boundaries and healthy thought processes will also be essential. These would be places where the individual who is undergoing restoration is not bombarded with temptation. This may very well include software to block inappropriate material from web browsers.

Like the spending journal suggested in dealing with those who have sinned through financial issues, journaling here will also be very helpful. Taking the time to work on a personal recovery journal and having an accountability partner or partners who have access to that journal to assist in the recovery. It will also take time to rebuild the damaged relationships, first with God and then with others involved. For those in leadership positions this may have far-reaching effects. First and foremost, the relationship with God will need to be rebuilt. There will be a great deal of shame that the offender may feel, and they will need to be reassured of the grace and forgiveness of God. "The gospel message of forgiveness has tremendous healing potential."[16] Beyond this, there is the rebuilding relationships with family members as well as those within the church community.

C) Emotional

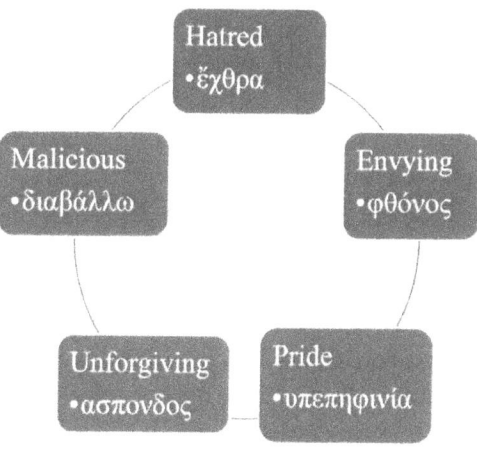

Figure 7: Connectedness of Emotional Sins

---

16. Yantzi, *Sexual Offending and Restoration*, 222.

Emotions sit at the core of man, yet a person's emotions are not the problem. Sin enters the situation when a person's emotions control them. The illustration in figure 7 emphasizes the interconnectedness of these out-of-control negative emotions. When one of these negative emotions is engaged it feeds both into the others and into itself. "Feelings, emotions, and moods constitute a river that continually runs through us—peaceful, meandering, turbulent, or raging—often beneficial, sometimes dangerous, seldom neutral."[17] All too often in life, people have the sense that their emotions are something that happens to them that they are not in control of, which is not the case. "Our emotional reactions depend on the story we tell ourselves, the running commentary in the mind that interprets the data we receive through our senses."[18] As life revolves around people, they respond according to what they understand. The problem is that the understanding is not always accurate. Of the current mythologies in working with the emotional makeup of an individual is REBT (Rational Emotive Behavior Therapy). "REBT's basic hypothesis is that our emotions stem mainly from our beliefs, evaluations, interpretations, and reactions to life situations."[19] Therefore, the story that people are telling themselves through self-talk is not always appropriate. People talk themselves into emotional responses that are counter-productive and often result in sin. A great deal more could be said concerning this issue, however the point is that much of the restoration needs of those dealing with issues in this area are outside the scope of the ministerial training of most pastors. Assisting people to realign their self-talk is best left in the hands of a therapist, the dealing with issues that may not have spiritual origins. Thus, it may be beyond the skill set of an individual to walk this person through the restoration process.

The outward expression of strife is at the time a mere reflection of the inner turmoil in the human heart. It is possible that this speaks to the ideas that stirred up the crusades as this would speak directly to those conflicts where theological themes were or are highjacked for the purposes of stirring up people. This would most likely be a cognitive rather than an entirely emotional issue. Strife may very well be reflected through what appears to be jealousy. Dealing with jealousy has ideological connections to anger and bitterness. While the emotional response to a situation might be jealousy, it will turn to anger, then bitterness. Jealousy is defined

---

17. Egan, *The Skilled Helper*, 79.
18. Williams et al., *The Mindful Way through Depression*, 21.
19. Corey, *Theory and Practice of Counseling*, 276.

by Aristotle as "the desire to have what another man possesses, without necessarily bearing a grudge against him because he has it."[20] While these two points are at odds, the fact is that they are both true and at the same time dealing with emotional instability. *Psychology Today* defines jealousy as "a complex emotion that encompasses feelings ranging from fear of abandonment to rage and humiliation."[21] To be given over to jealousy is to live "according to the flesh."

This speaks of desire out of context or control. Desire in and of itself is not a bad thing. The church is instructed by Paul to desire the better gifts of the Spirit (1 Cor 12:31). Envy is not just the desire but the feeling of wanting or needing something that someone else has that the individual feels they need or want. These two are intertwined with each other and may be better defined as narcissism and hedonism. These are like the two sides of the same coin. Because someone has an exaggerated affection for self they will deny themselves no pleasure. Scripturally this is viewed as the antithesis of those who are lovers of good (2 Tim 3:2, 3).

Ingratitude is seen as "a forsaking of God, taking only counsel from and for oneself."[22] So much of the attitude is focused inwards that there is little ability to turn outwards to have care or concern for others. It speaks of a life that is totally turned inward upon itself; one that has become self-sufficient has become like a god unto itself (Gen. 3:5). This is diametrically opposed to the growth that one is intended to have in Christ (Eph 4:24).

In appreciating the goodness of God, the believer is to put away all malice, and those attitudes that pull away from God. It is seen as lacking all virtue and social value.[23] The core of the person is mean-spirited with no godly affection towards others and an air of vindictiveness permeating the intentions towards another.

In dealing with many of the emotional problems that can plague man, one of the perspectives that needs to be considered is that of professional help. Mood disorders are covered to varying degrees in the *Diagnostic Manual of Mental Disorders*. The *DSM IV* lists mood disorders ranging from mild to severe with psychotic episodes.[24] While none of the emotions here that are listed as sin are listed in the *DSM IV*, they can be fueled by other

---

20. Brown, *New International Dictionary*, vol. 1, 557.
21. "Jealousy," *Psychology Today*.
22. Brown, *New International Dictionary*, vol. 1, 552.
23. Arndt et al., *Greek-English Lexicon*, 500.
24. American Psychiatric Association, *DSM-IV*, 20.

mood disorders. Should this be the case, most pastors lack the training for a proper diagnosis and would need to refer the individual to a therapist for assistance. Therefore, when dealing with any mood or possible mental disorders it would be wise to consult a family physician. If there are no underlying connections with mood, mental, or personality disorders, the patient care of a spiritually mature brother, sister, or pastor may be able to work with the individual to assist them in restoration.

D) Worship

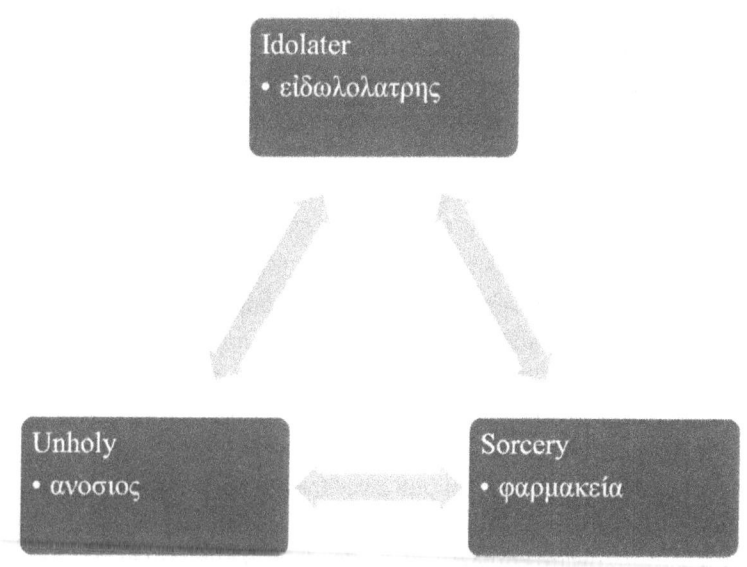

Figure 8: Relationship Between Sin in Worship

The first question in the *Westminster Shorter Catechism* inquires about the chief end of man. The response? "Man's chief end is to glorify God (1 Cor 10:31; Rom 11:36) and to enjoy him forever (Ps 73:25–28)."[25] This is what it is to worship, and yet there are sins that are related to worship in the word of God. Figure 8, like the illustrations of other sin categories, represents the interconnectedness of what we may call the subset of sinful activity. While engaging one specific sin doesn't necessarily lead into another in the subset, it may make it easier to fall into one of these other areas of sin. Some of these sins are such that they may require church

25. Westminster Assembly, *Shorter Catechism with Scripture Proofs*.

discipline for correction. Worship in contemporary churches is varied, from the more conservative churches that only sing the Psalms with no instruments to demonstrative services where the aisles are reserved for the dancers. Taking the teaching of Christ in the New Testament in stride, we are to worship the Lord in Spirit and in truth (John 4:23, 24). Sin enters into the situation when worship no longer has as its focus the God of creation, but on the creation itself.

The idolater is the one who has fixated their lives on any concept, person, object, or place other than the Lord. While this type of activity may be expected in the lives of pagans, it is not permissible in the lives of those who are called to be the saints of God. It consists of the displacement of God from his rightful place in the lives of his followers replaced by a cheap knockoff. The apostle Paul recognized that the objects of worship were backed by demonic powers (Rom 1:18–32). Now, if this were true in Paul's day, why would it be any less so in contemporary society? Whether an idol is a large bull, a horrific figure, a sports team, a screen, or a ride, it is the things in life that get in the way of God.

Sorcery or witchcraft is a mixture of the practice of "φηαρμακεία," that is, working with mixed potions, from which we get the word "pharmacy." The concept of sorcery is both the mixture of potions to dull the mind and the fallacy of being able to control spirits. "Even where magic deals with spirits as personal agents, it treats them as inanimate in the sense that they can be constrained and forced in an impersonal way rather than conciliating or propitiating them as in a religion."[26] There are only two types of entities that are spirit, those that serve the Almighty God and those that do not. Modern-day drug use may very well be dulling minds to the depth of spiritual realities, making those susceptible to the deceit that these realities do not in fact exist. For a follower of Christ to dabble in either of these areas—or any area that suggests a connection to spirits that does not include a dependence upon God—is in jeopardy of serious compromise of their walk with God. There may be a connection with this area of sorcery and those who have developed a false theology of controlling God by claiming the necessary format in prayer.

The Bible is clear that without holiness no one will see God (Heb 12:14a). That makes this area of sin especially damaging for the believer. The prophet Isaiah points out that all the righteous works of man are as filthy rags (Isa 64:6b), therefore the follower of Christ is utterly dependent

---

26. Brown, *New International Dictionary*, vol. 2, 552.

upon the cross. It is through the cross that an individual has access to "*Adonai Tsidkenu*," "the Lord who is righteousness." While holiness is a state of moral purity or perfection, a state to which man can never attain, unholiness for a Christian encompasses having abandoned the grace by which the righteousness of God has been granted them (Heb 10:29).

Unlike some of the other sin categories, those here under the classification of "worship," the church, pastor, and other leaders are uniquely qualified to handle—except for sorcery, the dealing with potions. The use and abuse of mood-altering substances are not part of the traditional ministerial training programs, however, as the abuse of these substances is on the rise, consideration should be given to familiarization with this area. Idolatry is an issue that the people of God have been dealing with from the beginning of time in the form of fertility cults and false deities. Little has changed. There are polytheistic and monotheistic religions reaching to the far corners of the earth and they are now all readily available through the internet right in every home with a computer, or radio, for that matter. It requires taking the time to carefully walk people through the Scriptures to help them understand the unique relationship that man was intended to have with God. What the cross made possible in the realization of this relationship, including what it means to walk with God.

E) Cognitive

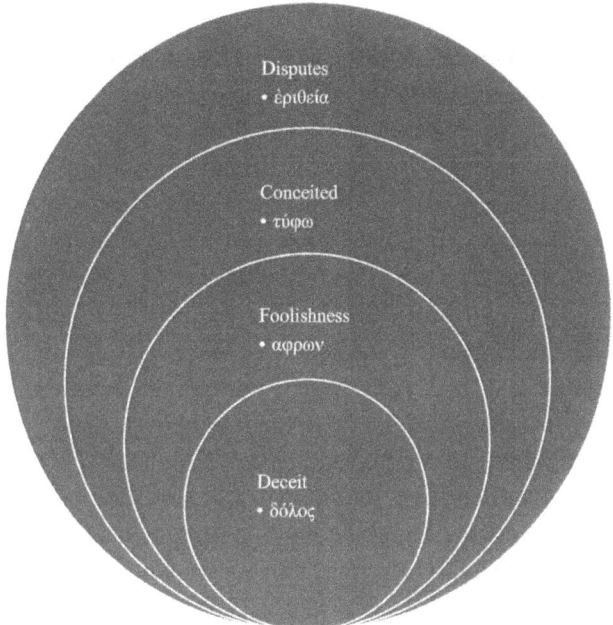

Figure 9: Development of Cognitive Sin

"For as he thinks within himself so is he" is how Prov 23:7a reads in the NASB, strongly suggesting that thoughts proceed actions. There is a contextual connection that restricts this passage, yet it doesn't take away from the overall message, that life springs from the mind. "We can understand cognitive processes as the procedures we use to incorporate new knowledge and make decisions based on said knowledge."[27] On these decisions, people act either for good or ill.

The core of these two issues is similar, those people who stir up problems. The graphic in figure 9 illustrates how deceit is at the core, whether that untruth is shared outside of oneself. As the individual believes a lie, the foolishness spreads, conceit can protect the lie. They are at the heart of divisions, stirring up one group against another. These are also seen as evil deeds in opposition to the efforts of Christ, especially seen as actions, working from a personal decision. While this may seem to be a neutral concept it has been used by Homer to suggest the tearing apart, to divide

27. CogniFit, "Cognition and Cognitive Science."

to separate.[28] This, by that very definition, sets itself at odds with the calling together of the church.

The heart of this concept in numerous European languages is to "lead astray" by one's behavior or words.[29] The notion is also caught up in treachery, most often used in an apocalyptic sense when dealing with false teachers. The use of deceit in the New Testament is always in reference to theological meaning.[30] The point is that this is never simply a matter of dishonesty; it is a matter of serious theological dissent, breaking from orthodox teachings and thus needing correction.

This is not merely a term that relates to the understanding, the ability to think, but to an individual's deficiency in moral attitude and disposition. "The understanding, namely, the faculty of religious discernment, is what is meant in Eph 4:18 by *dianoia*. Here we read of the darkening of the understanding—parallel, incidentally, to the futility of the *nous*."[31] This is the opposite of the ability to comprehend religious or spiritual truth.

This would be defined as the empty view of oneself, the sense of being inflated over against the actual nature of lacking substance. The threat of becoming full of oneself is a significant concern when choosing someone who is not yet ready for leadership, as per Paul's instructions to Timothy (1 Tim 3:6). It is an overly exaggerated sense of self-worth that sets itself over against the knowledge of a saint dependent on Christ.

This is specifically the area that Christ was addressing in the Sermon on the Mount, "anyone who is angry with his brother . . . " (Matt 5:22). He continues, "anyone who looks on a woman lustfully . . . " (Matt 5:28) shall be guilty as if the deed is done. An argument could be made that both situations are dealing with emotions, however, the cognitive choice is made to dwell on them. So, it could be argued that this text refers to a three-fold breech, encompassing sexual, emotional, and cognitive classifications of sin. Christ made it clear, "For out of the heart come evil thoughts—murder, adultery, sexual immorality, theft, false testimony, slander" (Matt 15:19). Each of these transgressions are born in the mind prior to the action taking place. It might be said that the primary battleground against sin is the mind. What must be taught, and people need to understand, is that "we are in the flesh, but we do

---

28. Brown, *New International Dictionary*, vol. 1, 533.
29. Brown, *New International Dictionary*, vol. 2, 457.
30. Brown, *New International Dictionary*, vol. 2, 459.
31. Brown, *New International Dictionary*, vol. 3, 127.

live according to the flesh. We live in the Spirit."³² The transition to actually live according to the Spirit and no longer according to the flesh is to grow in the Spirit. Gordon Smith suggests one possible discipline to assist this growth is to develop a sense of spiritual accountability, that establishes an accountability structure with those who are in a sense a spiritual authority in our lives, and through committed contemplative reading. "Spiritual accountability can be exercised through spiritual reading—the careful, meditative reading of the devotional or spiritual classics."³³

F) Activity

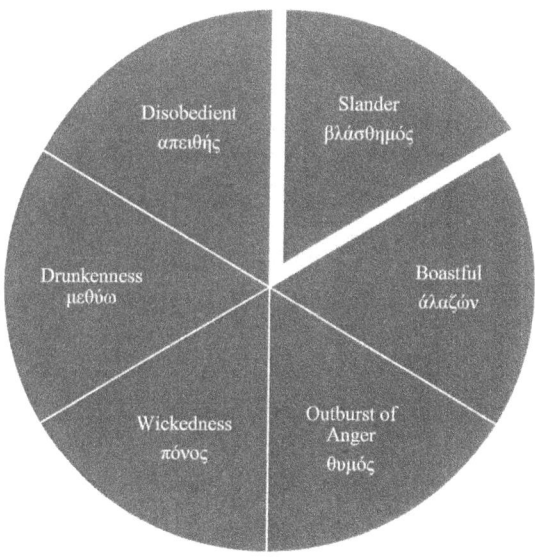

Figure 10: Common Core of Sinful Activity

Those activities that surface in life are the result of the various issues that are being dealt with below the surface. A common saying is that "the eyes are the reflection of the soul." Possibly a better rendition of this would be to say a person's actions are the reflection of the soul. This makes the actions of man both the cause and the effect of sin in life. Viewing the illustration in figure 10 one can see that these various sins, while distinct, have a common core.

32. Smith, *On the Way*, 40.
33. Smith, *On the Way*, 114.

The activity of an outburst, which is related to rage, is connected to pride, which is set over against the honor of God. Rather than being an expression of a God-honoring attitude, this is an action that literally dishonors God and is an insult to the Spirit of grace.

Wickedness is often seen as the "personification of evil or the devil in men."[34] The concept of wickedness was that of lacking something in the humanity of the person, in contrast to a good person who had no lack in this area. This conveys a sense of moral decline. In the New Testament, this may have some aspect of spiritual weariness that could very well be connected to compassion fatigue or burnout. This is a very real threat to those in the community of faith and especially those in leadership.

The fruit of the vine, while being an important part of the economy of the ancient Near East, posed a real threat to the lives of those who consumed it. The abuse of wine—or other alcohol—is seen as the cause for numerous evils. Its abuse was denounced by the prophets, and priests were to abstain from it during their temple duty. The abuse of wine is often seen as the gateway to a disastrous route in life (Prov 20:1; 31:4–5; Rom 13:13; Gal 5:21; Eph 5:18; 1 Pet 4:4).

This, in many aspects, would have connections to the sin of conceit, boasting overly of oneself. Original sin is seen in the context of glorifying self over against the knowledge of God, and as such thinking that God is unnecessary for one's life. In this sense, the boast would begin in the heart and convince the individual that they are enough without God, that in their own self-sufficiency, their own greatness, they need nothing more beyond themselves. The opposite of this can be seen as the correct attitude, that is to boast righteously, which would be to boast in God or in our weaknesses in contrast to God (2 Cor 12:9).

There is a wide range of misuse of speech that relates to this section. To begin with, there is a sense that those who were using words in this way were attempting to utilize some form of magical powers to affect the relationships between people, things, and other people.[35] It has to do with having a hostile attitude towards one's fellowman and towards God. Originally the term had no religious context in its usage. It was simply meant as a form of abuse.

The sense conveyed concerning being disobedient is to be out of step with the Spirit, in a way being in a spiritual wilderness, a desert that is

---

34. Brown, *New International Dictionary*, vol. 1, 561.
35. Brown, *New International Dictionary*, vol. 3, 340.

devoid of life, where one is subject to demonic dangers. It also connotes an attitude of rebellion or bitterness of spirit against the Lord. The result of this disobedience is a list of attitudes that the Christian is to put off (Eph 4:31), not acquire.

The author of Ecclesiastes states: "There is a time for everything, and a season for every activity under the heavens" (Eccl 3:1). However, this hardly includes activities that are an offense to God. The text goes on to list numerous activities that man can fill his time with to avoid the callous sinful activities as listed above. All but one of these activities may be resolved through teaching, pastoral counseling, and accountability partners. Each of these activities may have underlying causes that may require assistance and resources outside of which the church is able to provide. Drunkenness is an example and may reflect an alcohol addiction and thus require resources outside of the church. This is not however an excuse for the church not to get involved and make every attempt to come alongside and correct a brother or sister in Christ.

Addiction

One of the issues that must be addressed in relation to sin is the problem of addiction. Resolving a sin issue in the life of a saint takes on an entirely different set of components when an addiction is involved. Addiction is all too often overlooked in the addressing of sin in a believer's life. "Addiction is a condition that results when a person ingests a substance or engages in an activity that can be pleasurable but the continuation of which becomes compulsive and interferes with ordinary responsibilities and concerns, such as work, relationships, or health."[36] Simply rebuking a person with an addiction may not yield the results desired in a disciplinary process. This is an avenue within the context of church discipline that will definitely require professional assistance. Addiction isn't even level across the board. According to the American Psychological Association's website, genetics plays a role in the cycle of addiction. "About half the risk for addiction is genetic."[37] With this information, now how does a brother or sister in Christ approach or rebuke an erring saint? Especially in conjunction with a genetic predisposition to addictive behavior, how does the approach of the church need to be altered to best address the need of a sin-encrusted heart? At the same time,

36. "Addiction," *Psychology Today*.
37. American Psychological Association, "Addictions."

those involved in the disciplinary process with people displaying addictive behaviors need to keep in mind the following: "Addictions refer to a broader class of behaviors of habit or compulsion, such as sex, gambling, eating and so on."[38] As the church works with those whose behavior has gone to the point of compulsion and or addiction, greater care needs to be taken as these brothers and sisters may need more care and assistance.

Conclusion

This venture through hamartiology has not been for determining the extent of the offense, rather, it has been an examination of what may be going on inside the heart to determine the best possible treatment to bring the patient back to health (Gal 6:1). When a doctor suspects cancer in a patient they order the appropriate tests to determine the type, location, if it has spread, etc. to determine the most conducive course of treatment. Dealing with cancer, which can often be a life-threatening condition, is not a simple, straightforward, one-size-fits-all treatment. How then can we treat the serious issue of sin in the life of a believer, which is the cancer of the soul, with a simple one-size-fits-all restoration plan?

We need to familiarize ourselves with what happened in the life of the individual/the back story, prior to the unacceptable actions when beginning to consider the options in developing a restoration program for an individual. The more relevant information that is in the hands of those who are working to restore a brother or sister in Christ, the better. Understanding what went wrong, and how it went wrong, are the first steps in the process. This is where treatment begins. Establishing a plan for an effective restoration of the individual(s) involved is crucial. It begins with making sure that the right people or person is in place to care for the individual. After all, dealing with a brother or sister caught in sin is not like dealing with a fish caught in a net. The purpose is not to haul them ashore, gut them, and throw their entrails back into the sea, but to restore them to fellowship that the world might finally see that "glorious church without spot or wrinkle, washed in the blood of the Lamb." [39]

---

38. McRay et al., *The Modern Psychopathologies*, 183.
39. Hudson, "A Glorious Church," refrain.

Chapter Five _____

The Restoration Team

THERE IS AN OLD African proverb that states: "it takes a village to raise a child." Community plays a large role in the lives of the individuals. But what role does community play in church discipline? Simply put, everything. A person can stumble into sin on their own—although some sins require the participation of at least one other person. It is far more beneficial to have more than just one other person to rely on for the restoration process. A community, a team called together for the express purpose of rebuilding the fallen. The concept of a team is well established within the healthcare community. Bringing together teams of specialists to consult, treat, and provide aftercare for those in dire need is becoming or already is a standard practice. Following this wisdom, several authors suggest a similar structure to assisting those within the Christian community who are in dire need. "In the life of every church, there are times when individuals or families have spiritual needs that go beyond the scope of care usually provided by the church."[1] While this is not meant to exclude the local church, it opens up the field to include the entirety of the universal church.

In discussing support and accountability in working with offending members, Mark Yantzi suggests: "a support accountability group provides a safe and comfortable place for the individual to share."[2] When Dr. E. Wilson was forced to face his own entanglement with sin, he began his road to recovery in contacting a group to assist him that eventually became his "Spiritual Care Team."[3] In describing his take on the team approach to the restoration, Mark Lauterbach states get "a group of qualified

---

1. Wilson et al., *Restoring the Fallen*, 11.
2. Yantzi, *Sexual Offending and Restoration*, 143.
3. Wilson et al., *Restoring the Fallen*, 36.

friends."[4] For the purposes of this discussion, this team will be referred to as the "Restoration Critical Care Team," or RCCT, a team that responds at a critical time to care for the fallen and assist in their return to spiritual health. Recruiting for the team may be best suited from within a local church. However, drawing this team together should not exclude calling upon members from the larger community of faith who may also assist in the restoration process.

Proverbs 15:22 states, "Without consultation, plans are frustrated, but with many counselors, they succeed." Wise counsel and heeding the words of the wise are constant themes in the book of Proverbs. So why does the church abandon this practice when dealing with those who need the strength and resources of their spiritual community the most? There is a divergence between the rash actions that an individual might follow in contrast to the wisdom of a group. Having a group that can speak with wisdom and grace into a situation can assist in restoring a life in Christ, "implying a wise deference to the opinions of the wise and good, contrasted with rashness."[5] Rashness, that is, the swift and easy road, is not always the best or safest route (Prov 14:12; 16:25).

God has been calling together a community, not merely a collection of individuals, a group that is interconnected, interdependent. The question with which Cain responded to God, "Am I my brother's keeper?" (Gen 4:9e), remains the same today. All too often in churches where saints are struggling against sin this question rings throughout the sanctuary. The answer is the same today as it was when Cain shouted it out. Each one of us is responsible for those in the seats around us. It is to this end that the church is referred as the "body of Christ" (1 Cor 12:27; Eph 4:12) and the "family of believers" (1 Pet 2:17). Paul, in his instruction to the church in Galatia, stated that one who had been caught in sin was to be restored by those who live by the Spirit. They were to bear each other's burdens, fulfilling the "law of Christ" (Gal 6:1–2). "A new command I give you: Love one another. As I have loved you must love one another. By this everyone will know that you are my disciples if you love one another" (John 13:34–35).

Based on the new commandment to love one another, those that make up the church must therefore assist each other especially in areas such as recovering from sin. The question then is: who is it that Paul was talking about in Gal 6:1 that is to live according to the Spirit? It seems that the best

---

4. Lauterbach, *The Transforming Community*, 178.
5. Jamieson et al., *Commentary Critical and Explanatory*, vol. 1, 396.

person for the job is not a person but a team—specifically a team that is committed to the loving restoration of the individual who has had a sinful compromise in their lives. Is that not what the church is really for? The discipleship of those both prior to and following an encounter with Christ? There are also those who may not be committed to Christ who may be able to speak into a life that has been ravaged by sin and assist in their restoration. For instance, medical doctors and therapists who may not be people of faith may have insight into some of the related issues that the individual undergoing restoration may be dealing with.

In the book, *Restoring the Fallen*, which is written by a team of authors, one of them, Earl Wilson, recalls his journey of being confronted with sin and the restoration program that followed. The other authors consist of his wife and some of the members of the team that came together to assist in his restoration. This book will provide the backbone of this chapter. The accounts of Earl and the team that supported him provide invaluable insight, both into the development and the structure of a restoration team. As Wilson States,

> Sometimes a serious physical illness can land us in the hospital's intensive care unit (or ICU). A Spiritual Care Team is another kind of ICU. It is a group of mature Christians who voluntarily commit themselves to support and assist a person or persons with acute spiritual needs through a process of returning that person to fellowship with God, family and fellow believers.[6]

Putting together an emergency response team to assist a fallen brother or sister in getting back on their spiritual feet is no small task. Careful thought must be put into who those members will be who make up the team as these individuals will at times hold the lives of others in their hands. Once a team is called together, it should remain together as long as the restoration of those involved in a specific sin require, that is until they are released from their restoration. Even after the release of the individual, having some form of informal communication with the team and the restored individual may prove an effective accountability network.

---

6. Wilson et al., *Restoring the Fallen*, 11.

The Composition of a Team

Who then would make up this restoration critical care team for the wounded? This team will need to be made up of the best possible people on hand, which may not always come from the same denominational groups. It may very well be in the working out of the various theological gaps between denominational groups that wisdom is found for the fallen. It is time that many put away the walls that divide the body of Christ and come together to be the agents of grace that the Savior has called them to be. The offender's pastor should take the lead in putting together this team, though having some input from the offender would not be a bad idea. However, the offender should not have the final word concerning who is selected to serve in this capacity. The best possible situation would have everyone as a part of the same church. Some may be drawn from outside of the specific church that the offender attends as mentioned above, drawing upon the resources of the larger community of faith.

When putting together an RCCT, there will be a number of skills and attributes that one will want to see on the team, the most important of these being the spiritual attributes. While the natural mind of man is not always able to discern the things of the Spirit accurately, the Scriptures always stand as a guide. In leading God's people Moses called for help, "Choose some wise, understanding and respected men from each of your tribes, and I will set them over you" (Deut 1:13). There are three points that were to set these men apart from the rest. They were to be 1) wise, 2) understanding, and 3) respected. In the New Testament, those men who were chosen to provide leadership were to have two qualities. "Brothers and sisters, choose seven men from among you who are known to be full of the Spirit and wisdom. We will turn this responsibility over to them" (Acts 6:3). When these two lists are merged, the list becomes 1) wisdom, 2) understanding, 3) respected, and finally, 4) full of the Spirit.

Determining the maturity level of a given individual in these four areas is difficult. There is no inventory that a person can sit down to and fill out, which would provide a grading system for wisdom that might have as the most "The Wisdom of Solomon" (1 Kgs 4:29), and as the least, the "Foolishness of Nabal" (1 Sam 25:25). Even if that were possible, it might not be entirely helpful in setting the parameters for an RCCT. Now, this was just the first of the four parameters listed in the Old and New Testaments for the leadership of God's people. Surely those who are able to provide leadership to God's people should be sufficient to assist in a saint's restoration. To determine if an individual has any of these qualities to any degree would take familiarity with the person. Yet this team may require more insight as the restoration progresses.

While the aforementioned group may well cover some of the biblical requirements, others may be needed from outside the community of faith. In most cases, those being restored should advise their family doctor of their situation. Even when dealing with problems that seem to have less of an impact in a person's life, issues such as depression, anxiety, and any other mood disorders could surface during this process. As this may be the case, a professional therapist may also be a helpful part of the team. The first may be necessary to obtain the services of the second. Some therapists and registered clinical counselors will likely require a referral to be added to the team. While the idea of a restoration team will very likely be unfamiliar to those outside the community of faith, with the correct authorizations they will likely become valuable members. To share information amongst the team concerning the client/patient, the individual will need to sign forms authorizing the exchange/sharing of information.

For those required to step away from their careers for a time, there may be insurance that provides a possibility of recovering lost wages. For instance, when the sin involves a church staff member in a compromising situation, they may need to (temporarily) step down from their position of ministry. They may also require the help of a professional counselor or some form of legal advice. Most often it would not be necessary to have a lawyer as part of the restoration team, but it would be wise to consult with one or include one if the situation required legal advice.

Fitting the Need

Other issues to consider in the selection of an RCCT would be two-fold, namely, the nature of the offense and the response from the offender. At first this may not appear to have much bearing on the selection of the team; however, these two points are some of the most pertinent. This, and matters that will be discussed in the next chapter are the reason for the review of sin that was discussed in the last chapter. For example, an individual who has been discovered in an adulterous relationship would need a team of a different composition than a person who had engaged in some form or alcohol use or idolatry. The issue with alcohol abuse could very well lead to "drunkenness," alcoholism, or a recognized addiction. This may be the same with adultery, but this may be related to a sexual addiction. Wilson admits that the sin that he needed to address had evolved into a full-blown case of sexual addiction. The team that he needed included four confidants, a therapist, and a lawyer, these six people in addition to his wife.[7] Dealing with sin is not something that would be easily resolved, nor would it be pleasant. The point is that the restoration of different issues will at times require people with different skill sets.

Considering the various groups of sins that were listed in the previous chapters, different team members would be required in dealing with a person who has regular angry outbursts as opposed to someone who has been swindling—although the angry outbursts may very well be an individual's way of struggling with the convicting power of the Holy Spirit concerning a sin that they may have become tangled in. One sin might be a smoke screen for another sin. Working within a team environment will be crucial to working this through. When people are running scared, they have tendencies to do things they normally would not. Even those who have been discovered and have responded positively may still have some sin that needs uncovering. While working with the team that has been called together, complete disclosure is one thing that should be continually pressed for. The nature of this type of disclosure or confession will be discussed in greater detail in the next chapter.

Therefore, the nature of the sin that is being dealt with should have some influence and or effect on the structure of the team. If dealing with any form of addiction, it would be wise to have someone either on the immediate team or as a resource for the team to consult with that can speak to the concerns of addictive patterns. Even though various types of addictions will have some common elements, each will also have unique aspects that will need to be addressed. If possible, locating individuals to work on the restoration team who have the skills to deal with at least the known sin, will assist in the process.

As different people are being considered for a team, another point to keep in mind is how the offender responded to the various attempts to call them from their sin—i.e., whether the person approached others to confess their sin, thereby yielding to the conviction of the Holy Spirit, or if it had gone further to the point where the sin had to be exposed to the church. The

---

7. While the therapist and the lawyer are listed as members of the restoration team that Dr. Wilson listed, it was the first four, his confidants and his wife that were the primary members. There was not mention in the book as to his therapists' and lawyers' position concerning faith.

THE RESTORATION TEAM

process of discipline may have even gone to the point of exclusion from the assembly. The point at which the offender is ready to turn, confess, repent, and submit to a restoration program will affect the makeup of the team. While a group of very merciful individuals would be best suited for those who respond to the wooing of the Spirit, for the more resistant offenders a team made up of "firmer" individuals would be best-suited to the help that they may require; those who are unwilling to let the offender under restoration take any shortcuts or ignore any unconfessed sin.

Seeking out the various people in the setting of a small rural church may not be easy. It would be wise, if this is the situation, to locate the written resources that may inform the team of the base skills they may need to deal with the current sin situation.[8] Earl Wilson recommends that a pastor not be part of the restoration team, yet in a smaller church, this may not be an option. However, it would be wise to consider the reasons that Wilson put this forward:

- The time commitment is immense, and few pastors' schedules can absorb that much additional output.
- The potential exists for more than one Spiritual Care Team functioning at one time within a church.
- The family in crisis needs the pastor to fulfill his pastoral role with them, and that may be compromised if the pastor is part of the team.[9]

These are all very valid points, the last of which is the most significant of the three. However, the need for pastoral care on the team itself may not be avoidable. Work in the ministry is messy at best, and at worst, suffice it to say that the pastor is usually present for the best and worst times in peoples' lives. Unfortunately, all too often the best times can also run concurrently with the worst.

Making the issue of having a pastor as part of the team, or at the very least having an active presence on the team more complicated, may be the pastor's understanding of church discipline. Earl Wilson, in speaking with one pastor, ran into an opinion that was not entirely helpful. The advice he was given was neither helpful nor what he needed to hear. "He told me

---

8. Resources may possibly be located in public libraries; pastors may have some valuable resources in their own personal libraries. Internet searches may turn up a treasure trove of valuable resources. Caution should be taken with some resources located on the internet as these may not always be entirely reliable.

9. Wilson et al., *Restoring the Fallen*, 39.

not to disclose anything to the church. He also advised me not to share any more details with [my wife]."[10] Pastors bring a wealth of experience to the table dealing with issues like this, both from dealing with them during their ministry, as well as in the countless hours discussing issues in preparation for ministry. However, in this specific situation, it illustrates the need to wade through all the advice that will be offered and choose which to act upon and which to discard.

Voices

Within a team environment, there are a variety of voices that may all speak to a situation. Each voice brings to the team a valuable set of insights, experiences, and skills. Apart from the team environment, the number of voices would be significantly reduced. This may speak to the possible involvement of those who are from outside the local church as they would provide an objective voice in the restoration process. In his book, Earl Wilson shares the account of an observation that came from one member of the team set around him. "A few weeks into the restoration process, Virginia phoned me. We talked about some hard things. 'You must not be suicidal,' she said, 'if you were, you surely would have chosen to escape the pain.'"[11] The varied voices in the team provide the best possible opportunity to ask some of the hardest questions. Granted, in the case of Earl, Virginia commented, but this is a question that needs to be asked. "Are you considering harming yourself or taking your life?" While some may feel these are hard questions, even those considering the level of honesty that the individual who is the subject of the restoration is exhibiting, this question concerning harm or suicide is by far the hardest. Depending on the nature of the sin, and the mental/emotional state that the person is in, it may need to be asked more than once as the restorative process progresses. Some may think this is an unnecessary issue, after all, since a Christian would supposedly never consider suicide. But it is time for the church to think again. According to the World Health Organization, suicide is a leading cause of death on a global scale with almost 800,000 deaths every year attributed to suicide.[12] Those going through a restoration process will be very susceptible to depression, this alone increasing the risk of suicide exponentially.

10. Wilson et al., *Restoring the Fallen*, 75.
11. Wilson et al., *Restoring the Fallen*, 64.
12. World Health Organization, "Suicide Data."

Consider a Christian who has just come face-to-face with sin. They have been confronted, and regardless of where in the confrontational phase they have confessed, all too often they are treated as weak or traitors. "The world often views discipline as the expression of anger and hostility, but according to God's Word, proper discipline is the expression and outworking of love"[13] (Prov 10:12; 1 Cor 13:4–7; 1 Pet 4:8). The reason the world sees this as an expression of anger and hostility is the way the church often reacts. This needs to change; more sermons concerning the ever-present reality of sin need to be preached. The people of God need to be reminded that none are completely without sin (1 John 1:8). John was not writing to those outside the community of faith but to those inside of it! "The church has been accused, sometimes rightly, of shooting its wounded and abandoning those whose behavior is less than exemplary."[14] The team will need to watch for signs of depression and make sure that appropriate steps are being taken as necessary.

Dealing with issues that result in shame may be akin to playing hopscotch in a minefield. People's emotions come into play which makes dealing with sin that much more difficult. It would be nice if correcting sin in the life of a believer was as simple as dealing with an error in computer code. While the team keeps this shame within the group, with more people knowing the depths of the shame this also provides for a greater number of voices supporting and loving them. It is true that people deal with shame differently. Yet through the grace of God shame is undone (Rom 10:11). Shame is a difficult emotion to handle, yet God uses it for his purposes. "But in keeping with the Gospel, this intentional shame is redemptive and merciful since such shame results in godly sorrow, which in turn, points us back to Christ, who bore our shame and guilt and set us free form the wages of sin."[15] Shame is a powerful emotion, much like conviction, it will either drive to despair or to grace. It may very well be the voices in the RCCT that help the individual who is the subject of the restoration to process the feelings of shame and depression in a healthy/positive manner.

---

13. Laney, *A Guide to Church Discipline*, 29.
14. Wilson et al., *Restoring the Fallen*, 12.
15. Cheong, *God Redeeming His Bride*, 149.

Conclusion

Dealing with sin is not a pleasant or easy thing. If "going it alone," one is often defeated and overwhelmed. When this happens, all too frequently the individual falls back into the sin they were trying to escape. Recurrently in Scripture, the entanglement of sin is metaphorically referred to as "mire," a thick clay-like mud (Ps 40:2; 69:14). This is a great comparison, as the more a person struggles to get free of sin/mire, the more deeply they become bogged down/entrapped. For one person alone, it can be hopeless to obtain their freedom, yet with a friend, a partner at one's side, the journey becomes easier, and recovering from sin and failure becomes a greater possibility (Eccl 4:9, 10). Those who are confronted and must deal with their sin, having someone, even the one who confronted them, come alongside to assist, makes the difficult days ahead more bearable.

While it would not be wise to give strict guidelines on the formation of an RCCT, having the ideas that are mentioned throughout this chapter in mind will assist in the formation. Strict guidelines are only as useful as well drawn-up battle plans—which are usually not useful beyond the first contact with the enemy. (It seems someone always forgets to inform the enemy of what it is that they were anticipated to do.) After that, pandemonium breaks loose, nothing works, both sides admit that it was a mistake, and everyone picks up their weapons and goes home. Unfortunately, that is not how life works. Because people are involved, as well as the fact that life tends to get messy, it is better to have a broader set of guidelines.

Even with a broad set of guidelines, often it is not the guidelines but the people that need to be considered. Who is better to choose, a secular therapist or a church janitor, who understands at a deep level what it means to walk in the Spirit and has a compassionate, gentle heart? It could be this person, the one that seems the odd one in the group that will all too often point out the missing pieces. And who is ministering to those in the "impact zone," the family members or church members who have been pushed off to the side and forgotten, whose lives, hearts, and faith have been shattered? While the one under correction gets the help needed, who will be there for those left in a state of spiritual shellshock?

Very often those from the impact zone are missed/bypassed as the restoration progresses. As the discussion now moves into the restoration process, there will be some space given to consider the lives that are affected by the sin of a loved one. Various matters will be brought into the discussion for consideration. With the variety of sins discussed in chapter

4, it should be apparent that a one-size-fits-all restoration program will not work. Grabbing a sinning saint, slapping them on the forehead, screaming a loud prayer, and instructing them to sin no more will most likely not be effective in any case. There will be several things to consider when developing an effective program for the individual caught in sin. A program built for them, considering their sin, and taking into consideration those in the "impact zone."

The end result of the restoration process should be the saint caught in sin once again walking in humility and confidence in God; a life that has various disciplines in place to safeguard against sin finding a foothold again; and the people from the impact zone cared for, loved, encouraged, and walking closely with their Savior. Restoration is not meant to return things to the way they were; rather, it is meant, over time, to make things better. A weak spot has been repaired, a life strengthened, sin dealt with. There may be pain in the journey, disappointment, and frustration; however, the desired end result is a more confident walk with Christ.

Chapter Six

Repairing the Bricks

> As you come to him, the living Stone—rejected by humans but chosen by God and precious to him— you also, like living stones, are being built into a spiritual house to be a holy priesthood, offering spiritual sacrifices acceptable to God through Jesus Christ.
>
> —1 Pet 2:4–5

IN THE TEXT ABOVE, Peter refers to the people of God as "living stones" that God is using to build a "spiritual house." Anyone in construction will attest to the fact that on a work site, accidents happen, and material gets damaged or destroyed. A damaged brick is of no use in a wall, and there will either be extra bricks on hand or a quick trip to a supplier. Through a local supplier, a standard brick will sell for less than a dollar. But what Peter means by these "living stones" is different. These stones have been purchased at a much higher price, the very blood of Christ (cf. Acts 28:20c; 1 Cor 6:20a; 7:23a). This means that the value of these stones is incalculable. Therefore, to extend the metaphor, every effort must be made to examine damaged stones, determine where the weaknesses are, and restore them for their use in the wall of this "spiritual house," which is the craftsmanship of the Almighty God. As the discussion develops throughout this chapter, a broad-based paradigm for restoration will be reviewed—a broad-based paradigm in that there is no sequential pattern given in Scripture to follow like those for discipline laid out by Jesus and Paul (Matt 18:15–17; 1 Cor 5:1, 2; Titus 3:9–11), working towards a holistic and adaptive restoration model and including points essential for spiritual development that may be applied in numerous situations.

So, let us consider a scenario with an individual who has been confronted regarding their sin and is being cooperative. A team has been called together and is aware of the unique issues concerning the sin at hand. The process is ready to get underway and the restoration of the saint to begin. Questions to consider are: who creates the plan? What is the next step? At what point will this process be complete? While navigating through the often-turbulent waters of restoration there are at least two comforting thoughts. The first is that this is not uncharted territory. Others have gone on before, and it is therefore possible to learn from both their successes and failures. The second point is evident in the following quote. As a follower of Christ, one has the leading of the Holy Spirit to lean on (Prov 3:5–6). As Earl Wilson writes, "Though none of us had a master plan or even a well-formulated view of what restoration entailed, the team was committed to looking to the Spirit of God to lead us, to gleaning truth from Scripture and to seeking wise counsel."[1] Few, if any, start this process with clear direction. There are many things that can either go awry or so well that plans become virtually ineffective.

So then, without clear direction, no plan or map to follow, how does the RCCT and the individual subject to restoration move forward? There are steps that need to be in place for a successful restoration of the individual(s) involved. But it must first be determined what restoration is. As Laney explains:

> In classical Greek the verb "καταρτιζο" had a wide variety of meanings which can be gathered under one of two headings; (1) "to adjust, to put in order, to restore"; (2) "to equip or fully furnish someone or something for a given purpose.... The basic meaning of the word is to "restore to its former condition.[2]

Restoration is to give the entangled believer the opportunity to return to the liberty that they had in Christ. Jeschke adds to the understanding of the task at hand: "In discipline, as in the presentation of the Good News to a non-Christian, a person is presented the opportunity of being liberated from the power of sin in all its forms by coming under the rule of Christ and walking in His way."[3] This entails taking the liberty that is afforded through the cross and again joining in fellowship with God and the community of the saints.

How does a person who has injured their soul restore it to its former condition? While there are several places in the New Testament that provide some direction in discipline (Matt 18:15–17; 1 Cor 5:1–5; Gal 6:1–5;

1. Wilson et al., *Restoring the Fallen*, 34.
2. Laney, *A Guide to Church Discipline*, 85.
3. Jeschke, *Discipling the Brother*, 181.

Titus 3:9–11), there are not any that deal with restoration (Gal 6:1; 1 Pet 5:10). It may be that there are no guidelines given because each person is so very different, and each restoration needs to be navigated with the offender in mind. As Dr. Wilson and the team began their journey to walk with him as he rebuilt his relationships, with God, his wife, family, and close friends, he admits they had no direction other than the leading of the Spirit. "None of us had a master plan or even a well-formulated view of what restoration entailed, the team was committed to looking to the Spirit of God to lead us, to gleaning truth from Scripture and to seeking wise counsel."[4] The following pattern gives a brief guide that is flexible enough to be applied in most situations. As this process moves forward there are several points that need to be considered:

- Confession/Disclosure
- Repentance/Forgiveness
- Assistance
- Acceptance/Reinstatement

Working through these points should provide a functional yet adaptable process that should be equally useful in most situations. This is not intended to be an entirely exhaustive set of points to cover. Rather, the intention of bringing these into the discussion is to provide a starting point/springboard to launch the restoration of the individual. There may be other considerations and other additions to this list where the function would support the redemptive nature of the restoration.

Confession

Leeman lists the principal purpose of church discipline as bringing sin out of the shadows into the light. "First, discipline aims to expose. Sin, like cancer, loves to hide. Discipline exposes cancer so that it might be cut out quickly (see 1 Cor 5:2)."[5] Confession needs to take place at the beginning of the restoration, because until the offender confesses, it remains nothing more than an accusation, and still a matter of discipline. Once the offender has brought the sin out of the shadows, then, and only then, can the restoration move forward. Even at this point, the RCCT will be able to assist the

---

4. Wilson et al., *Restoring the Fallen*, 38.
5. Leeman, *Church Discipline*, 33.

offender. The temptation will be there to only divulge that which is felt to be necessary. Dr. Wilson links this to the offender giving consent and submission; however, the confession needs to precede the consent as the offender needs to admit his/her need first. Scripture is clear that no one is without sin and secondly, confession is required (1 John 1:8, 9).

The number of people who may need to know of the confession is dependent upon the stage of discipline at which the individual responded, as well as those affected by the sin. If the offender responded to the conviction of the Holy Spirit and the impact zone of their sin is limited, then the only people who really need to beware of the confession would be those who received the initial confession and those affected. In talking about this very issue amongst those on his restoration team, Dr. Wilson mentions that "the need for confession is clear. The question of how widely the confession should extend must be sensitively explored."[6] If during the disciplinary stage the offense became widely known, then the confession will need to have some form of public acknowledgment. Again, this will need to be handled with sensitivity. The RCCT should have all the "gory" details, as they will need to address the extent of the sin and see to the repentance from it, and the offender's restoration. The more public announcements will need to be managed with care, especially concerning the nature of the sin involved. It would be very prudent not to mention the names of anyone else involved in the public announcement, even if people were co-offenders. Everyone that may have been involved in the sinful activity needs to address their issue(s). Consider the following two hypothetical scenarios, to place some of this discussion in context.

Scenario A: Consider a situation where an individual has been caught in the midst of sin—and let us say the sin at hand is swindling, which was discussed in chapter 4. What kind of confession would be required to consider the person as a restoration candidate? This would be a person who is so aggressive in the obtaining of financial gain that they are willing to "trample upon the needy" (Amos 8:4). The impact zone of the sinful activity is wide-reaching; people affected are both those on restricted finances and those who have ample financial means. With different people being impacted by the original sin is it possible for a complete restoration without those affected being acknowledged in some form through the confession? It might be wise to create various levels of the confession that would specifically address those in various levels of the impact zone. Every painful detail

---

6. Wilson et al., *Restoring the Fallen*, 74.

would need to be included, bringing the full scope of the sin into the light. In the copy for those on the restoration team, it would be advisable to list each victim and the amounts that were involved for each.

Requesting this type of acknowledgment would have a two-fold influence on the situation. First, it would communicate to everyone involved the sincerity of the confession, both in the details and those that the confession is extended to. Second, it gives the offender no place to hide; sin is exposed and so will need to be dealt with. It would be a definite asset to have a lawyer to consult with at this point regarding these confessions, concerning what needs to be included and what not to include. (These letters could very well be used in a court of law, and some adjustments may need to be made for that.) There is no place in the Bible that suggests that even a repentant sinner is free from the natural consequences of their sin. At the same time, it would be prudent not to make matters worse than they need to be. How bad can things get? There are times when dealing with sin that situations will get very bad, but sometimes these things need to happen. Legal cases may need to be pursued, criminal charges may be in order, consequences need to happen. The confession needs to clear the heart of the offender in order that grace may flood in.

Scenario B: A small group member is promoting ideas that are contrary to orthodox theology. Let us say he is teaching that when Christ was on the cross, he was not God, that somehow, he had given up his deity since it is inconceivable that God could die. There are numerous sins that may be involved in this action. One may consider foolishness, or the denial of the divinity of Christ, as this goes directly against the teaching of the Bible (John 1:1, 14; Rom 5:8). There is absolutely nothing that would suggest that Christ on the cross was any less God. The apostle John recognized that Jesus was God (John 1:1, 14, 18). Paul also recognized that Jesus was in fact, God (Col 2:9).

The confession in a case such as this would need to take place, preferably in a group setting, with each person attending the small group meetings present. It would be advisable for the leader of the restoration team to provide some type of breakdown concerning the errant nature of the teaching. It may be necessary/useful to make the church aware that there had been some erroneous ideas introduced in a small group that are being addressed. The structure of the confession presented to the church would need to be less detailed. Bringing a confession at this level may clear up any residual effects of the teaching as well as confirming Paul's instructions concerning elders (1 Tim 5:20). While the teacher may not be an elder, it may be considered an elder responsibility, and as such be treated in the same fashion. Also, it provides the church the opportunity to see—to a lesser degree—the process played out before them. Specifics would not only be unnecessary but potentially harmful. The aim is always to bring the person to a point of restoration.

All too often people try to cover over sin, in the hopes of protecting the name of the church and the sinner. After all, the Bible itself teaches that love covers sin. "Above all, love each other deeply, because love covers over a multitude of sins" (1 Pet 4:8). This passage, however, was never meant to convey that love would turn a blind eye to sin, but rather that love continues for the sinner regardless of sin. This is evident in its most powerful expression. "Greater love has no one than this: to lay down one's life for one's friends" (John 15:13). The reality of this is seen in the cross through which the power of sin was broken, and life was made available. This is the point of restoration, namely, to call those who have offended back to life.

The idea of the various levels of confession has a three-fold purpose. First, to protect those in the impact zone from any further pain. Secondly, to provide only the information which is both helpful and pertinent to the restoration process. Thirdly, to bring the sin out into the open where it can be dealt with. There is evidence that in the early church this idea of a multi-layered confession would have been entirely foreign and rejected. Studies into the patterns and practices of the early church suggest a far more aggressive approach to dealing with sin: full public disclosure.

> The indications of all the early literature are that confession in the first centuries was public. In fact, the clergy opposed private confession and insisted that sins confessed in private should be made known publicly. This included all sins, both those sins committed in secret and those already known to the public.[7]

Confession needs to take place, and it needs to be done at a significant level, assuring that as many people who need to receive it do. Whether or not one appreciates the concept of the fully open and public confession or not, one can see that it would disable hidden sin's ability to cripple the saints and the church. However, a truly open confessional environment in the church might not work at this time. The current ethos of the church may be far too disjointed thereby potentially proving to be detrimental

---

7. Wilson et al., *Restoring the Fallen*, 74.

to the health and life of the church. Confession in a written form should begin with the RCCT. From there, as the need is determined, it should be edited and given to those who have had the unfortunate experience of being in the impact zone. Once the RCCT is confident that the entirety of sin has been exposed to the light, they can then begin to work out what repentance might look like.

Repentance

The next step in the process of restoration is repentance which is contingent upon confession. "Produce fruit in keeping with repentance. And do not begin to say to yourselves, 'We have Abraham as our father.' For I tell you that out of these stones God can raise up children for Abraham" (Luke 3:8). The point being made is that confession is the cause, and repentance is the effect; however, the continuing development of the confession is the evidence of the effect. Before a person can repent, they need to at the very least admit or confess to themselves and God that there is sin in their lives. There is no alternative to repentance: it is essential. That is, as soon as the confessor begins to acknowledge the sin, it needs to stop. This is what repentance is: "a change in actions resulting from a change in convictions."[8] Whatever the individual is doing, repentance is to stop the action or to start doing what they aren't doing—i.e., taking responsibility for their thoughts, behaviors, or actions if they had not done so previously. While confession needs to precede repentance, it is not that the repentant attitudes and actions wait; rather, once the confession begins, repentance follows immediately on its heels. There is no waiting for its incorporation. The process of working out the entire confession may take weeks to months since facing up to one's guilt and shame is not easy. However, as soon as the development of the confession starts, repentance needs to follow.

As the confession begins to develop and the magnitude of all that has run afoul in the offender's life comes into focus, the areas that require change also begin to emerge. Dr. Wilson lists five points that need to be a part of repentance:

1) Sin must be acknowledged as sin,

2) bridges need to be burned,

---

8. Laney, *A Guide to Church Discipline*, 92.

3) the possibility of sin must be ruled out,

4) there must be a willingness to allow other sin to be brought to light, and

5) repentance needs to be understood as both an event and lifestyle change.[9]

Providing a brief overview of this list will open up the discussion on repentance.

1. Acknowledging sin. This phase of the restoration is meant to take the time and recognize the entirety of the sinful activity, not just the sin that was discovered but any other activity that was included as well. Part of human nature is to attempt to sidestep responsibility. God questioned Adam concerning what he was hiding. Adam tried to shift the blame and avoid responsibility (Gen 3:12). In a similar way, when God inquired of Cain concerning his brother Abel, Cain tried to avoid taking responsibility for his actions by attempting to evade the question (Gen 4:9). The pattern begins there and continues to the point where man thinks he can lie to the Holy Spirit (Acts 4:3–4). When sin is not recognized and acknowledged, the tendency is to remain in that state. Repentance is to acknowledge and turn from the sinful state. "True repentance assumes responsibility without excuse, the phony kind makes excuses."[10] Repentance begins with standing up and taking responsibility for one's actions.

2. Burning bridges. Certain relationships need to be ended if authentic repentance is to be engaged. An adulterer cannot maintain a relationship with the person that they engaged within adultery. An alcoholic cannot visit his old drinking buddies (unless they are abstaining as well) or visit a bar. There are certain relationships and/or activities that must be discontinued. "When I was stood up for a social or business engagement or finished the engagement early, I'd use the extra time to feed my sexual sin."[11] There needs to be a voluntary breaking with those aspects of life that have the potential to lead the offender back towards their sin. This may very well be a very painful experience; family-wide friendships may be affected. When an affair occurs

---

9. Wilson et al., *Restoring the Fallen*, 66.
10. Lauterbach, *The Transforming Community*, 147.
11. Wilson et al., *Restoring the Fallen*, 70.

between two parties of close family friends the burning of bridges will have an effect on everyone in the impact zone, the entire families of both offending parties.

3. Ruling out sin. In talking about burning bridges, it is referring to those relationships that can draw a person back into a sinful pattern. In this section, it is taking the time to analyze habits and routines to discontinue any behaviors that could possibly lead to a return to the previous sinful behaviors. That is, to determine in as much as is possible, to remove anything that might lead back to the sin. Paul, in writing to the church in Ephesus regarding teaching against giving the devil a foothold, states, "Anyone who has been stealing must steal no longer, but must work, doing something useful with their own hands, that they may have something to share with those in need" (Eph 4:28). Paul instructs them to find ways to avoid the sin. For instance, in the case of stealing, to alleviate the need by working and having enough to provide for others, that they will not be tempted.

4. Willingness for all sin to be brought to light. When caught in a sinful activity that requires the intervention of church discipline, all other sinful activities associated with that activity will need to be exposed. As Dr. Wilson notes, "A turning point in the whole process came when Virginia asked, 'Is there anything else you need confess? If you are going to clean house, you need to sweep the corners clean.'"[12] Dr. Wilson admits that he wanted some of his sin to remain hidden, that he did not want to add to the shame and struggled with God concerning disclosure. "The whole truth was that I was giving in regularly to a sexual addiction—not only the affair but also the use of pornography and visits to massage parlors, prostitutes, and nude bars."[13] He had to acknowledge that, "Secrecy kills; only truth heals."[14] To move forward in the restoration, there needs to be a clean slate, as residual sin can hinder the process.

5. Repentance as an event that starts life change. Repentance is when a choice is made to abandon the entangling sin and pursue a different course. Life patterns need to change. This may include seemly innocent activities, such as the route one takes home. For a saint struggling

---

12. Wilson et al., *Restoring the Fallen*, 25.
13. Wilson et al., *Restoring the Fallen*, 26.
14. Wilson et al., *Restoring the Fallen*, 54.

against drinking, a route past a favorite bar could be disastrous, just as going past an adult video store would be for sexual sin. "True repentance is essentially a desire to think, be and do differently."[15] The point is the desire. This is at the heart of repentance; a change in the desire of the heart which affects the entirety of life.

With the real change beginning at the heart level, it is difficult to measure the change that may be taking place in the heart. As the Pharisees and Sadducees came out to where John was baptizing, he challenged them. "Produce fruit in keeping with repentance" (Matt 3:8). While the entire conversation is not recorded here, what can be taken away is that repentance will produce fruit. Determining what this fruit will look like is in direct relation to the sin that is being repented of. For example, scenario A listed earlier in this chapter described an individual who was guilty of swindling. Fruit of his repentance might take the form of voluntarily submitting all his financial record to a forensic accountant for inspection. It may also take the form of working toward compensating those who were taken in by his sinful activities. Fruit would take the form of some type of legitimate evidence supporting the efforts toward repentance.

The members of the RCCT would be the ones who would be best able to measure the fruit of repentance. Working with the individual where the purpose of the team is to ask the hard questions gives them unique insight into the person's life. It is often through the hard questions, that the fruit of repentance is revealed. Again, regarding working out the confession, the process of repentance and the fruit evidencing the repentant heart may take months to work out. At no time should any of the restoration process be rushed. It is the heart/core of the person's being that is being worked on before the cross of the loving Savior. Trying to rush through any part of church discipline, or the restoration process, will do more harm than good. When Peter and the other apostles were brought before the Sanhedrin for preaching in the temple courts, Gamaliel, the very man who instructed Paul, recommended patience to let things work themselves out (Acts 5:34–39; 22:3). If the advice that delivered the Lord's disciples out of the hands of the Sanhedrin spoke to letting time run its course, then should the church not take note of it and follow it today?

---

15. Adams, *Handbook of Church Discipline*, 44.

Assistance

Discussing the assistance that may be needing to be provided during the restoration process may be a shorter discussion than that of the two previous points. The reason being that some of the assistance rendered will have taken the form of working through the confession, assuring that it misses nothing, and to whom it needs to be confessed. It also includes working through the entire concept of repentance, which may begin in a moment of tearful reckoning, but will be worked out over months and perhaps years to come. Much of this will have been worked out with the RCCT, as the team helps the saint find his way through the labyrinth back from the muck and mire of sin. Also, depending on the nature of the sin, how far along the disciplinary process went before the erring saint yielded, and how many people were aware of the sin, the group providing assistance may grow dramatically.

Jay Adams points out that all too often churches neglect the assistance that the saint undergoing restoration needs, which results in the saint falling back into their sinful habits.[16] In order to keep the saint from falling back/regressing into destructive habits, the people of God need to come together and support the struggling person. But what kind of support is needed? Again, this often depends on the sin which the offender was involved in, the extent to which the disciplinary process needed to go, and the attitude of the offender under restoration. One of the first points mentioned by Dr. Wilson is a safe place. "In too many churches it is anything but safe to be authentic about our life situations."[17]

Where else in life should people feel safer than in their own homes, that, and possibly their home church? But what does one do when the church is no longer seen as a place of safety? Too often the church has more in common with the Sanhedrin than with the living body of Christ. A false sense of righteousness and holiness are displayed as many forget that their righteousness is like a filthy rag (Isa 64:6). It is only our absolute dependence upon God that makes us righteous. Our strutting around with a false sense of self-righteousness is meaningless, a chasing after the wind (Eccl 1:2). The entire book of Ecclesiastes screams about the foolishness of our self-sufficiency. The end of the matter, Qohelet tells us, is to fear God and keep his commandments (Eccl 12:13). We are to keep

---

16. Adams, *Handbook of Church Discipline*, 95.
17. Wilson et al., *Restoring the Fallen*, 128.

his commandments, the second greatest commandment being to love our brothers as ourselves (Mark 12:31). The responsibility of the church to provide a safe place for sin to be confessed and dealt with is of the highest priority for the people of God. One key element in establishing this is the constant reminder that people are broken and damaged by sin and entirely dependent upon the saving grace of God.

Following safety, another area of assistance that may need to be provided is counseling. This may very well take a different approach than the guidance provided by the RCCT. Consider the issue of an adulterous affair. Even if the offending member of the marriage has responded to the church's rebuke (regardless of the level), has confessed, and is showing clear fruit of repentance, the marriage may still be in danger. The couple may need marriage counseling and support. If the confession has impacted other members of the family, then this may require the assistance of family counseling. Dr. Wilson's daughter had the opportunity during an informal meeting with members of her father's Spiritual Care Team (what is referred to in chapter 5 as Restoration Critical Care Team), to receive healing herself. After a tearful conversation with members of this team, she was able to turn to her father to say, "Daddy, I've forgiven you, and I don't hate you, but it just hurts so bad."[18] The member under restoration is not the only one who needs assistance and support. Everyone in the impact zone needs care.

People may need help in establishing new patterns of doing things. Consider the individual from scenario A, the individual caught swindling others out of their earnings and futures. It is possible that this sinful pattern has become so intertwined with their basic business philosophy that he/she may not be able to function apart from it. Should this prove to be the case, it will be necessary to help the individual to construct an entirely new business ethic. Within the church itself, there may or may not be the resources for such an endeavor. (Not every church has proficient business personnel. Someone may, however, know where these skills may be obtained.) The situation in scenario B is an entirely different scenario. Correcting flawed doctrine is an area that the church should be able to handle. This, after all, is part of the purpose of the word of God. "All Scripture is God-breathed and is useful for teaching, rebuking, correcting and training in righteousness, so that the servant of God may be thoroughly equipped for every good work" (2 Tim 3:16–17). Teaching and correcting are directly in line with dealing with false

---

18. Wilson et al., *Restoring the Fallen*, 88.

teachers in the church. So, dealing with the individual in the second scenario is specifically in line with the purpose of the church.

There are numerous forms of assistance that the church can provide for the person being restored. Adams points out that this is something that needs to be suited to the individual situation.[19] Each person and situation must be examined by the church; the sin is dealt with, and the scope of those affected all need to be measured. Again, a cookie-cutter approach will do more damage than good. If the church has been active throughout both the disciplinary and restoration processes, then it should have a fairly reasonable grasp on the situation and how to best come alongside those involved. The final stage of restoration is the acceptance back, and complete reinstatement into fellowship—first with God and secondly with his church.

Acceptance/Reinstatement

The most important aspect of this entire project of church discipline and restoration is to restore to fellowship those who have become estranged from God due to sin. The clearest sign of successful restoration is said so well in that old hymn, "Just a closer walk with Thee." However, measuring an individual's personal walk of faith is not entirely possible, yet as the hymn above recognizes, the deep heart desire to be closer to God is a good sign. Dr. Wilson notes: "Spiritually, I had begun to learn to be comfortable in God's presence: praying, reflecting, sitting still."[20] This marks the formal end of the restoration process when fellowship is restored first with the Savior and then with the people of God. Granted, forgiveness is available the minute the saint confesses and cries out to God, yet at times trust must be built up again. People need to be reminded of this reality. In speaking of the fullness and completeness of Christ's sacrifice Bayer recalls: "Thereby he gave to all who believe, as their possession, everything that he had. This included: his life, in which he swallowed up death; his righteousness, by which he blotted out sin; and his salvation, with which he overcame everlasting damnation."[21]

The salvation that was purchased on calvary is fully realized once again and life instead of death guides the sinner home. As with salvation, this is something that the individual must work out on their own. Guidance may be offered, the text of Scripture and its application to life may

---

19. Adams, *Handbook of Church Discipline*, 95.
20. Wilson et al., *Restoring the Fallen*, 153.
21. Bayer, *Living by Faith*, 49.

be explained, but it is up to the individual to "seek the Lord while He may be found" (Isa 55:6).

The acceptance and reinstatement of the fellowship of believers may be somewhat more complicated. The heart of man is hard and full of corruption, including those within the church. Accepting back a fallen brother or sister may be difficult for some to deal with, especially if they were present in the impact zone. They may need help in accepting back this individual who caused them such anguish and discomfort. Yet forgiveness is not an option for the people of God. It is obedience to the word of God to extend the grace that has been received to those who need it most. More than a group of righteous people, the church should be known as the forgiven and forgiving. A similar format to that which was used in the announcement of the sin should be used in the formal reinstatement.

For some, there may be little to no impact. If the restored offender was not involved in many ministries, it may simply be a matter of welcoming them back to the communion table if they were publicly rebuked or expelled from fellowship. It might be a symbolic gesture to have them serve during the celebration of the Lord's Table. Depending on a church's tradition, this may take the form of handing out the elements or reading a text of Scripture. All restrictions should be lifted at this point and the individual should once again be free to celebrate with the church.

Although the requirements of both Scripture and the church may be met, there may be requirements of a legal nature that may continue to be in place. Also, the church may not be able to address certain issues if the involvement in the sinful situation had any professional consequences, such as violating codes of conduct of a professional organization that the individual may be affiliated with. (A letter of recognition from the leadership team may or may not be helpful.) Certain restrictions may be imposed by authorities outside the church that should be observed, such as if the case involved a minor. These restrictions will need to be reflected in the church. Reinstatement does not mean that the consequences of one's sin are removed. There are times when the consequences will have to be endured regardless of what may be worked out in the life of the believer.

Conclusion

The one supreme guiding principle for the restoration of the fallen is from Paul's letter to the church in Galatia: "Brothers and sisters, if someone is caught in a sin, you who live by the Spirit should restore that person gently. But watch yourselves, or you also may be tempted. Carry each other's burdens, and in this way, you will fulfill the law of Christ" (Gal 6:1–2). The key points from the text are "you who live by the Spirit" (those who made up the RCCT) "restore that person gently." As Dr. Wilson points out, "It doesn't say restore him quickly. It says restore him 'gently.' Gentle restoration takes time."[22] This is part of the ministry of reconciliation that the church is called to (2 Cor 5:18). The reconciliation extends to those who, because of the entanglement of sin in their lives, may be in full flight away from the presence of God. This may have some resemblance to the story of Jonah, with the exception that it is sin, not a whale, that swallows the believer. The way out is still the same, confession, and repentance (cf. Jonah 2).

Restoration is complete when the individual is released by the members of the RCCT and the leadership of the church to re-engage in community life. This may include the opportunity to once again be active in any number of ministries within the church, or to represent the church to the public at large. The conclusion of the process should be determined by a written agreement between the RCCT and the leadership of the church. These would be those who have walked through this process with the individual. They would have the clearest insight regarding the spiritual, emotional, and mental standing of the restored member at any given point in the restoration. Should the RCCT feel comfortable in releasing the individual from the restoration process, the church should take note and act on this, re-instituting this individual completely.

The completion of the restoration should not be to simply cut the individual loose. It would be prudent for the church to establish some form of a formal accountability structure to assist the saint in staying away from the sin that lured them. "The need for accountability after the formal restoration process is finished should not be overlooked—it is critical."[23] The possibility of harmful practices and patterns resurfacing once life returns to normal is highly likely. The only real safeguard left—other than the deterrent of having to go through this process again—is being held accountable by someone who is familiar with the person's previous struggle and is there to journey alongside to keep the sin in check.

A basic pattern for the restoration of a brother or sister who has been caught in sin has been discussed here. In dealing with a member of

---

22. Wilson et al., *Restoring the Fallen*, 34.
23. Wilson et al., *Restoring the Fallen*, 154.

someone in a position of trust or leadership, there are additional points to be considered, along with the issue of working within denominational structures that will guide the restoration process. Those in leadership have an added burden concerning the issue of trust. To return to a position of leadership, this trust must be re-established in such a way that the sin(s) having been addressed will not interfere with the future of the individual's ministries. Chapter 7 will discuss some of the unique aspects that those in leadership will have to grapple with, especially those who wish to re-enter the ministry at some point after being restored.

Chapter Seven

Broken Trowel

CHRIST CLEARLY STATED THAT he would build his church and the very gates of hell could not withstand it (Matt 16:18). In the building of his church, he has likened people to living stones (1 Pet 2:4). That being the case, what is possibly the most used tool in the hands of a stonemason is the trowel. The trowel makes a good metaphor for those in leadership—pastors, elders, and deacons. The trowel is used to put the cement in place and set the stones, aligning them with the other stones according to the master's plan. This is the purpose of the assigned leadership in the church: to build up the church (Eph 4:11–13). The problem is that tools, like the bricks themselves, get damaged and must be repaired or replaced. An actual mason may make a quick trip to a local hardware store to replace a broken trowel. This is where the similarity ends; if the bricks for this spiritual house are priceless then that extends to the tools as well.

Restoring/repairing people is not always pleasant work. Paul wrote to the church in Galatia that those who are spiritual are to restore those caught in sin. To successfully walk with a person through the restoration process takes time, often difficult, heart-wrenching moments when life struggles against the lingering damage of sin. Those in any form of leadership are often placed on a pedestal and when they fall off, the disgrace is at times expressed far too harshly. Very similarly to the previous chapter, the discussion here will deal with this process. Yet the application will be directed to those in various types of leadership while bringing into the conversation the various stages that will assist in the restoration of those who have been involved in leadership positions.

You know the trowel is broken when a leader in the church stands tearfully before the congregation and stumbles through a letter of confession. Another member of the leadership team steps up to try to make some sense of the situation that is unfolding before the church. A wave of sorrow and anguish sweeps across the sanctuary; the elder at the pulpit looks out and with a gentle voice starts. The elder acknowledges the confession, that a member of the leadership team was caught in sin and has submitted to the rest of the team. The elder goes on to explain that a plan is being developed to restore the wounded saint. A general sigh of relief sweeps over the congregation and hope begins to build. The congregation is reminded to avoid gossip, and if they have questions, they may approach members of the leadership team. They are encouraged to give the leader in question and the family some space to sort things out. The congregation is informed that the reason for this meeting is to fulfill scriptural principles in both the confession and restoration (1 Tim 5:20; Gal 6:1–2). The church should be informed that this public announcement also provides the opportunity to bring to bear the full resources of the body of Christ into this situation. With this, the meeting is brought to a close and the congregation is requested to keep this matter in prayer. The elder prays and the meeting is dismissed, people filter out, some stopping to briefly pray for the leader in question.

For the sake of this discussion, who in the church is considered a leader? A leader or member of the leadership team is anyone who may be in a named or formal position of authority—whether a teacher from the Christian education department or a member of the worship team. The primary leaders of the church are those on pastoral staff, and the elders and deacons. For some churches, there may be little difference between the elders and deacon boards; other churches may consider the pastoral staff as the elders. Here we will discuss three tiers of leadership in the church, in increasing degrees of responsibility. First, those who are in a visible form of public ministries such as teachers and worship leaders. In the second tier are those in foremost leadership positions, including elders and deacons and non-credentialed pastoral staff. The third and final tier is the credentialed pastoral staff of the church.

For the leader who is the subject of restoration, it may feel like the confession was the hardest part, but it is just the beginning. For the most part, the restoration process of one in leadership is like that of a layperson although with some additions. For those who are credentialed ministers, there will be denominational involvement. Different denominations will have diverse requirements for their credential holders. There may be others, including counselors, added to the church's RCCT list due to these requirements. The denomination will most likely have some criteria that must be met before the credentials (if credentials are involved) would be reinstated.

There will be numerous meetings between church and denominational representatives to assure that all the necessary steps are taken for the reinstatement of individual's credentials. It is highly likely that denominations may have some form of fund set up for counseling those in a situation such as this. There may be other resources at the denominational level that can be offered to the RCCT to assist in the whole process. These may include insight into other areas that will prove invaluable such as the experience of dealing with others in leadership positions that have led to both positive and negative outcomes. Every experience provides a wealth of knowledge and information for future encounters.

This discussion will move through the four points that were mentioned in the previous chapter; confession, repentance, assistance, and acceptance—not that these are the only points that may need to be addressed, rather these would be starting points and other considerations may be added to the process. As the leadership definition has already been broken up into three groups, designating them into three tiers may assist in clarity. Tier 1 would be those in public, visible ministry including but not restricted to Christian education teachers, Bible study and/or home group leaders, volunteer leadership. Tier 2 those in primary leadership roles such as deacons and elders and, finally,[1] tier 3 those in credentialed ministry positions, the highest responsibility and oversight level in a church. At each point, possible considerations will be added to the discussion as it relates to the different tiers. Throughout the discussion within this chapter, tiers 1 and 2 will often be combined as these two have more similarities with each other than with tier 3. The implications of the various phases of the restoration process mentioned in the previous chapter are certainly applicable here, yet in dealing with those in leadership, new/additional concerns must be considered.

Confession/Disclosure

It is inevitable that working out the confessional process with those in any form of leadership is a delicate endeavor. The higher the number of the tier of leadership, the more complications come into play. Regarding a person

---

1. For the sake of the discussion, elders in tier 2 would reflect those elected or appointed to an elder's board and not those in a credentialed position of leadership.

in leadership, it is important to give out an appropriate amount of information partly to communicate to the church that: a) the sin is taken seriously, and b) more importantly, so is the grace of God. Unlike dealing with the confession of a layperson who is not in a leadership role, dealing with the sin and confession of a person in any form of leadership needs to have a public component. At the very least this will hinder gossip and support the reality of the grace of God through the restoration process.

Tiers 1 and 2: Due to the nature of the public aspect of those in ministry, these tiers need to be included in the public confessional process. In many contemporary churches, an elders' board functions in a similar capacity to a lay pastor, sharing in the spiritual/ministerial duties with the pastor. The deacons' board often serves in a leadership capacity overseeing more of the non-ministry related activities such as food being passed out to widows (Acts 6:1–4). Whether they are selected and ratified or elected, these are persons in leadership positions. Simply put by Paul, those in leadership are to be reproved before everyone (1 Tim 5:20).[2] Depending on the traditions of the church involved, the specific sin and the cooperation of those entangled in sin, the confession may be delivered by the individual or any leader from tier 2 or 3. Elders and deacons form a unique layer of church leadership.

A confession at this level should contain a brief statement of moral or ethical failure, that the error is acknowledged and that appropriate measures are underway to correct the issue. Also, whether or not the individual was in submission to others in leadership, and that restoration is underway. The confession of a person from a tier 2 position would require more details and a greater level of transparency than that of tier 1. This needs to be guided by grace, wisdom, and a high level of propriety.

Tier 3: credentialed leadership, the clergy. The denomination may have requirements concerning the wording of the confession. It would also be very wise to seek legal advice depending on the sin which the clergy was involved in. The confession should be made by the individual, in person, to stand before the people that they have served and look them in the eye.

---

2. The term used in the text is *presbutevrou/presbuterou*, or presbyter, a leader in the early church. In the specific context the person is one who draws his livelihood from the church and ministry. Paul includes teachers alongside apostles and prophets on two occasions, placing them is a unique group of a common responsibility (1 Cor 12:28, 29; Eph 4:11). Finally the Letter from James notes the strict judgement for teachers (Jas 3:1). The contemporary church may see differences between lay and credentialed leadership. However, it seems that Paul and James do not share that opinion.

If there is any hope for the reinstatement of the credentials, the church will need to see the sincerity of the remorse. Redeveloping a sense of trust cannot begin too soon.

As with the laity, the confession at any of the tiers may require multiple versions, each with different levels of detail. The greatest amount of detail would be divulged to the RCCT and denominational leaders, then, less detail to any direct victims, and again, to a lesser degree to those in the impact zone who may need to know. Finally, the least amount of detail would be required for public disclosure. The varied levels are necessary as there are some that need to see the honesty yet not all the details in the confession. Seen in figure 11 each of the various tiers and the possible additional versions of the confession that would be required.

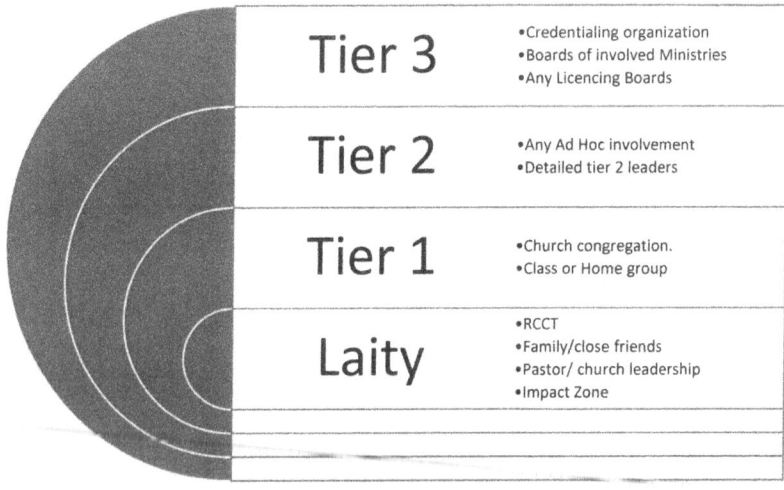

Figure 11: Confession Guide

Confession is a necessary part of working towards the re-establishment of the integrity needed to be reinstituted in a ministry position. Regardless of the level of leadership service, the rebuilding of trust is essential. The loss of trust is possibly one of the most damaging issues that needs to be dealt with before a leader can be restored and reinstated into a position of leadership and service. A complete and accurate confession is the first step to rebuilding that trust.

Repentance/forgiveness

Repentance begins the same way for those in leadership as for the laity. Even as the confession is being developed, repentance needs to ensue. It may be necessary to establish that some areas of repentance are in place prior to delivering the confession. Again, there will be several different elements that constitute repentance, some more measurable than others. The attitude of the heart is impossible to measure; however, there will still be the fruit of repentance.

1. Acknowledging sin. Each person who has been involved in some form of sinful activity needs to acknowledge that what they were involved in was sin. Dr. Wilson recognizes that acknowledging sin in a person's life is horribly painful but true repentance requires it.[3]

2. Burning bridges. Once the confession is complete, and all sin has been recognized and acknowledged, anyone else who may have been involved is named.[4] Any and all relationships with those who were involved need to be dissolved entirely. It would also be advisable to break off all unhealthy relationships. Part of repentance is to have a sense of regret over the sinful actions. This should be carried over to include a desire to break completely from everything and everyone associated with the harmful behavior.

3. Ruling out sin. If there was no pleasure in sin, there would be no temptation. In ruling out the possibility of returning to the sin, one is going a step beyond burning bridges, closing off the entire road. In the changing of one's mind and attitudes, the pleasure of sin may be seen for what it really is, bait for the trap. Ultimately, the best way to avoid getting caught is to avoid the trap. To avoid the trap the bait needs to be ignored.

4. Willingness for all sin to be brought to light. Regardless of the tier of those in leadership, the acknowledgment remains the same, there needs to be complete disclosure. For those in leadership, any hesitation may complicate the matter of being reinstated to any form of leadership in the future. It is a necessity to advise the offender of this prior to beginning the process of confession for the repentance to be

---

3. Wilson et al., *Restoring the Fallen*, 66.

4. These names should only be mentioned in the confessions that are for the RCCT and possibly those denominational leaders who are involved.

considered legitimate. Therefore, those offering the confession should be encouraged to take their time to be entirely accountable.

Repentance can be a difficult activity to ascertain. Often people expect repentant sinners to be carrying themselves in utter sorrow at all times. However, for many who are in a state of genuine repentance, a great weight has been lifted off their shoulders and they find peace with God. There are also those in various leadership positions that consider tears to be evidence of a contrite heart. If we consider the power of the Holy Spirit to convict (John 16:8) when true repentance takes place the heart will no longer feel the conviction but be at peace.

Assistance

Those in areas of leadership will need slightly different forms of assistance. At every tier, there will need to be assurances that life goes on beyond the failure. There may be a greater need to communicate this at the leadership level as the public disclosure will create a deeper sense of shame.

Tiers 1 and 2: For the most part, those in this group will often have their issues most easily addressed as a good deal of the support needed will be available from within the church, informing the RCCT, possibly with the counseling as well. Granted, recalling Adams' insight mentioned in the last chapter, churches all too often don't meet this challenge well.[5] When dealing with elders and deacons, things begin to get a little more complicated. Should any of the offenses brought against them be related to a financial offense, the situation will require legal advice. Tier 2 level of leadership often deals with the finances of the church, and an offending elder or deacon may have some hard questions to answer. Even as the assistance being rendered here is part of the restoration process, it does go beyond the restoration itself. "It would also be wise for an elder to be assigned to meet with the individual regularly for concentrated discipleship and counseling after that person has been reinstated."[6] In working with tier 2 leaders especially dealing with finances: "The person may need guidance in guarding himself against the same sin."[7]

---

5. Adams, *Handbook of Church Discipline*, 95.
6. Hammett and Merkle, *Those Who Must Give an Account*, 179.
7. Lauterbach, *The Transforming Community*, 174.

Tier 3: Even with an RCCT in place that is primarily made up of members of the church, a denominational involvement will most likely take the lead in assisting a credential holder. Depending on the sin involved, there may be other aspects in assisting a credential holder to rebuild the trust in the pastoral office as well as himself. Consider some of the following:

If the sin is that of adultery or some form of misconduct with the opposite sex.

1. Always have another person in the building when counseling a member of the opposite sex.
2. Install a door on the counseling office which prevents total privacy, such as a door with a glass insert, or a window.
3. Publish counseling guidelines, including counseling hours and days, with an acknowledgment of the extent and limits of individual training in counseling.
4. Create a referral list which is considered "safe," and actively make referrals to these professional therapists.
5. Decide in advance how much touching is appropriate and state in writing that hugging, holding hands, etc. is inappropriate.[8]
6. Ask the church to pay for the services of a mental health professional as a supervisor/consultant in counseling matters and establish regular times to consult with this mental health professional.[9]

There may be variants of these which would be applicable to other areas of sinful compromise. Consider the financial compromise. One variant may be to have the credential holder distance himself from the finances of the church by putting a human "layer" between the credential holder and the cash flow. Possibly a treasurer and/or an administrator who maintains the integrity of the cash flow, providing the credential holder a buffer between them and the handling of money.

The purpose of assistance is to come alongside a brother or sister and journey with them, bearing each other's burdens in love (Eph 4:2). As Lauterbach comments,

---

8. Having this printed in a larger font and posted on the office wall so that it is easily seen and read would be advisable.

9. Grenz and Bell, *Betrayal of Trust*, 144. Neither Grenz nor Bell attempt to define what "safe" from point 4 might entail, thus possibly finding gender specific or sensitive therapists should prove safe.

Instead, says Paul, reaffirm your love for that person, I believe this is where we fail, we forget that forgiveness is not enough. We are awkward with them and not sure what to say. Paul says: assure them of your love. Do it repeatedly. This man or woman is learning to walk again after a self-inflicted injury to their soul. They need support and help along the way as they regain confidence in their muscles. This includes everything from personal meetings for encouragement and prayer, to financial support or counseling.[10]

Those who are recovering from sin feel the crushing weight like no one else does. On the journey to the first meeting with some of the people that would form his RCCT, Dr. Wilson recalls the trip. "I boarded the boat as a critically wounded person. Unlike the boat, I was without a rudder and without a compass. I was adrift, panicked, still looking for a way out."[11] Part of the reason for assistance is to remind people that they are not alone.

Acceptance/Reinstatement

The final stage of restoration is to see the individual(s) being reinstated, similar to the laity, in the relationship with Christ, then to their relationships in the church, and finally, if possible, to the ministries they were forced to leave. Not everyone will be able to return to the ministries they left; for some that will never be possible. "For some offenders, including predators, restoration to leadership and public ministry will likely never be possible."[12] "This does not mean that the fallen will never be restored to the ministry of any kind, but it does say that 'full' restoration does not necessarily mean restoration to all forms of ministry."[13] This is the harsh reality of the natural consequences of sin. As the discussion looks to the reinstatement of leaders at the various tiers what needs to be applied is the effort to look beyond the relationship—which is by far the most important aspect—to the ability and opportunity to serve.

Tiers 1 and 2: Being restored to ministry will be dependent upon the evaluation of the RCCT and the elders in charge. Tier 2 level leaders will have to deal with even more scrutiny than that of the tier 1 leaders as they will be handling delicate, financial, or confidential matters of the church.

10. Lauterbach, *The Transforming Community*, 177.
11. Wilson et al., *Restoring the Fallen*, 24.
12. Grenz and Bell, *Betrayal of Trust*, 172.
13. Wilson et al., *Restoring the Fallen*, 165.

There may be some situations where returning to the public ministry may not be possible. However, if it is possible, every effort should be made to do so. Some may not want to return, but for those who do, it may be essential for them to know they can. Forgiveness is a powerful thing and should never be withheld. "While you must forgive in your heart and not carry bitterness against another, you may not *grant* him forgiveness (i.e., the promise not to bring up the matter again) until he repents."[14] This is why repentance comes before acceptance and reinstatement. To have gotten this far in the restoration process, there must have been fruit in keeping with repentance (Matt 3:8). Finally, re-establishing trust and confidence in the person is essential for the reinstatement of individuals at any level.

Tier 3: For credential holders to be reinstated they must have met the requirements of the denominational officers, along with the approval of the RCCT they were working with. As was said in tier 1, they may not be able to return to their former position. Again, this may be decided outside the church by the credential-granting denomination. A great deal of this depends on the nature of the offense and the initial response from the individual involved.

Conclusion

People tend to struggle with God, even as they begin to move through the restoration. "This is where Christianity gets uncomfortable, I found myself arguing with God and losing."[15] This was Dr. Wilson's lament prior to the development of the Spiritual Care Team that formed around him. While the concept of the care teams may not yet be widespread, they can be invaluable in the restoration of those entangled by sin. In an episode of the short-lived TV science fiction series, *Firefly*, one of the characters tells another: "when you can't run, you crawl; and when you can't crawl, you find someone to carry you."[16] This is the heartbeat of those who come alongside the person undergoing restoration, specifically the RCCT, coming alongside those who can't crawl and carry them to the finish line. A similar act was viewed by millions during the 1992 Olympic games. Derek Redmond, running in the semi-final of the four hundred meters tore his hamstring before he could finish the race. Waving off stretcher bearers, he struggled

---

14. Adams, *Handbook of Church Discipline*, 54.
15. Wilson et al., *Restoring the Fallen*, 33.
16. *Firefly*, season 1, episode 14, "The Message."

to his feet and hobbled towards the finish line. A man from the crowd of spectators ran, pushing past security, joined him, and helped him finish the race. It was his father.[17] This is the essence of a restoration ministry.

For the sake of the discussion, at this point, the restoration has been successful. The individual has returned to their former area of service, regardless of the tier. It may seem that the work is done, and that life may go back to normal, but support needs to continue. "There is little more to say about this aspect of discipline except to remember that to preserve the gains that have been made."[18] Accountability may need to go on for years beyond the restoration to assure that the restoration endures. In speaking to the value of accountability in the avoidance of sin, Laney states, "Personal accountability to a pastor friend has proven effective in my own life to help me avoid certain sins and temptations."[19]

Discipline and restoration are two distinct ministries, and they are vital ministries of the church. They are often missing in a functional aspect of many churches. Some churches have the discipline part down pat; however, the restoration portion is missing or not planned out. "I have seen restorations without a process. They either fail for having no benchmarks or succeed without apparent reason."[20] The restoration process needs to be as well planned out and executed as the disciplinary process was. While much of the process must begin on an ad hoc undertaking, as it proceeds it should build direction, intention, and a reasonable target for the completion of the restoration of a brother or sister in Christ.

---

17. Ward-Henninger, "Olympics moment."
18. Adams, *Handbook of Church Discipline*, 97.
19. Laney, *A Guide to Church Discipline*, 161.
20. Lauterbach, *The Transforming Community*, 195.

Chapter Eight

Occupancy Permit

WHY IS THIS CHAPTER titled "occupancy permit"? Peter tells us that Christ is building a spiritual house using his people as the materials and tools (1 Pet 2:5). The bricks are his people, the trowels, those in various forms of leadership in the church. There are times when on a construction site that materials and tools are damaged, yet the work needs to continue, so those damaged items need to be assessed and restored. Once the damaged items are restored construction continues and the wall in this spiritual house may be completed. When the wall is finished, and the building is ready for occupancy, a permit is issued as a declaration that the building is safe for human occupancy. While the spiritual house may not be quite done, the living stones and the trowels are all back in use. The construction continues. There have been setbacks, but the work goes on—after all, Christ did promise: "And I tell you that you are Peter, and on this rock, I will build my church, and the gates of Hades will not overcome it" (Matt 16:18). The point is that Christ will build his church, and nothing Satan can do will stop that, even including the "sin that so easily entangles" (Heb 12:1). Life happens, and people make mistakes that impact their lives, often needing assistance to get out of the mess that they get themselves into.

The discussion that has developed over the last seven chapters has been a journey through the restoration process, beginning with the discovery of sin in the life of a fellow believer. The process has been walked through right to the restoration of the saint if that is at all possible. There are times when people will not turn from their sins. At that point all the church can do is treat them as though they are pagans and try to reach them with the gospel again. In wrapping up this discussion, the church needs to be reminded that the saints of the living God are never disposable. Those who have fallen into error need to be challenged and whenever possible restored to the place that God has called them. The issue then is helping them find their way through the mire of sin and back to the place where they are restored to fellowship with God and his church, including any area of service that they may have been called to.

Jeschke comments in the opening pages of his discussion into the matter of church discipline, "church discipline is the task of discipling the faltering brother in the church."[1] Yet discipline is almost a lost art in the church; no longer does an older sibling in Christ walk a younger one through the steps of growing in Christ. Rather, now they are handed over to the pastor's class or a new believer study. "But most Christians today are not known for making disciples. We have developed a culture where minister ministers and the rest of the church sits back and enjoys 'church' from a comfortable distance."[2] It appears that the people of God may have lost the art of being the people of God. No longer do we give any thought to being our brother's keeper. It is easier for members of the community of faith to falter and stumble. Throughout this discussion on church discipline and restoration, there are few specifics and many general approaches. The reason for this is that it is difficult to presuppose all of the factors that may be involved in a saint stumbling into sin. This being the case, it would be unwise to prescribe a solution to a problem that is not entirely understood. As this discussion began the church was defined understanding the purpose and necessity of discipline within the community, as one would in a family. The problem all too often is that the community is becoming less of a community and more of a corporation. The centralized structure of many churches takes the responsibility out of the hands of the congregants and puts it into the hands of the experts. There is no argument that as a disciplinary process proceeds those in leadership, the "experts" may need to get involved. Also depending on the nature of the infraction, those in leadership may need to become involved. There are times when the problem needs the eyes, skills, and wisdom of a person who has the experience.

At times there may not be an experienced person around, then a person is needed who knows where to look for guidance. Henry Blackaby comments on what should be a very normative practice, not only for those in leadership but also in the daily life of the laity. "[Christ] had simply watched for the first sign of the Father's activity."[3] Often brothers and

1. Jeschke, *Discipling the Brother*, 4.
2. Chan and Beuving, *Multiply: Disciples Making Disciples*, 9.
3. Blackaby and Blackaby, *Spiritual Leadership*, 28.

sisters in Christ rush in to try to correct a flailing sibling in Christ without taking the time to think or pray it through. It was to this end that Christ taught his disciples to follow in his footsteps. "Likewise, he trained his disciples to watch for God's activity rather than to set their own agendas."[4] Dealing with sin in the church is a delicate matter and must be dealt with by the utmost care.

Looking to God

In the zealous desire to protect God and his glory the church often responds too swiftly and too harshly. The contrast is that very little is done, citing some out-of-context desire to avoid the whole issue. "Too often churches are weighted toward one or the other of these two extremes."[5] Part of the purpose of the discussion has been to prevent either of these extremes, to hopefully find a way somewhere between the two. To get to this place those involved need a change in perspective. That is, to put away the ideals of man and take up the purpose of God. This means that people are dealt with where they are at and not where others think they should be (Rom 5:8). This means engaging people at the point in their lives when and where they need assistance the most. "Engagement means we cease to minister at a safe distance, instead we touch people's lives."[6] Dealing with the lives of those people who have become snared in sin is neither clean, safe, or unloving.

Quite to the contrary, discipline brings cleansing to the soul, safety and peace to the heart, and is the ultimate act of love to an erring saint. "The world often views discipline as the expression of anger and hostility, but according to God's Word, proper discipline is the expression and outworking of love."[7] The love of God extends to man regardless of where he is, but that love is too great to leave men in the sin. "True spiritual leadership is taking people from where they are to where God wants them to be."[8] The heart of the matter is this, that it is the love of God that is the motivator for a church that disciplines. If it is legalism, then it is doomed to failure. "So, love should motivate all of a church's discipline."[9]

4. Blackaby and Blackaby, *Spiritual Leadership*, 28.
5. Adams, *Handbook of Church Discipline*, 92.
6. Lauterbach, *The Transforming Community*, 16.
7. Laney, *A Guide to Church Discipline*, 28.
8. Blackaby and Blackaby, *Spiritual Leadership*, 22.
9. Leeman, *Church Discipline*, 23.

When Discipline Fails

Discipline is not always successful, there are times when it fails, and sin continues and reigns in the life of a saint. "In almost half the cases where church discipline is administered, restoration fails to take place."[10] Laney provides several reasons for this, including only administering discipline in cases where there is a sexual offense, or when the issue is aesthetically displeasing, or what might be considered the "big" sins. Therefore, the earlier discussion from chapter 4 reviewed sin to understand its destructive power. "Jesus never encouraged us to ignore sin."[11] Sin separates, it damages, it violates. Yet others are left with no challenge because those around them feel inadequate to the task of correction.

Throughout the discussion in the previous pages has been a basic run through of what discipline needs to consist of to address the issues at hand, beginning with the complaint and the various approaches in the confrontation. Asking questions even before any "formal" disciplinary action begins may jolt a wayward saint to respond to the conviction of the Holy Spirit and confess the matter before they are confronted (John 16:8). The formal disciplinary action begins with the two private approaches, then on to the public approaches. There may be times when discipline needs to go the entire path laid out by Christ to the dis-fellowshipping of a saint until they (hopefully) return. The ultimate failure in the disciplinary process is when they fail to return and continue in their sin.

Sin is Sin

It needs to be acknowledged that many people in the contemporary world have an unspoken "sin scale" that determines, in their own minds, which are the bad sins, and which are the not-so-bad sins. Consider the following results from a study conducted by the Barna Group:

> There are huge gaps in between young believers and older Christians when it comes to the acceptability of sex outside of marriage, profanity, drunkenness, pornography, homosexual sex and illegal drug use. The only two areas of statistical similarity between older

---

10. Laney, *A Guide to Church Discipline*, 150.
11. Wilson et al., *Restoring the Fallen*, 14.

and younger born-again Christians are views on abortion and using the f-word on television.[12]

So, for example, sex outside of marriage is permissible but not swearing on television. But sin needs to be understood as a violation, as a destroyer of fellowship, of relationships. The sin scale needs to be set aside and the reality of the nature of sin accepted. There is no minor or major sin, no cardinal or venial (allowable) sin, if you break part of the law you break the whole law (Jas 2:10). Sin can kill, John is clear about that (1 John 5:16, 17), but it need not kill the saint. However, it does disrupt the rich fellowship between saint and Savior, between siblings in Christ.

Putting sin back into perspective is necessary for this discussion. There are a few volumes that have been produced dealing with church discipline, mostly sexual misconduct in the pastorate. This gives an unhealthy picture of the body of Christ; it is not only those in the higher tiers of leadership in the church that need to be chastised and only over what some feel is the only significant offense. To the contrary, sin needs to be dealt with, all sins, and the erring saint corrected. It is not until sin is understood for what it is that its true danger is understood. "Yet sin is not merely wrong acts and thoughts, but sinfulness as well, an inherent inner disposition inclining us to wrong acts and thoughts."[13] Sin dwells in the heart of every living human being, regardless of faith. Everyone struggles with it, and when a sibling in Christ is overcome by it, the instruction from Scripture is clear: restore them (Gal 6:1).

Construction

Repairing, rebuilding, and restoring the lives of those who have been run over by sin is no easy task. The road back into fellowship with God can be a rough one. Through the discussion on the previous pages, the task of restoration was broken down into two groups, the laity and those involved in leadership. Those involved in leadership positions in a church are again broken down into three tiers, as the contemporary church has a more complex leadership structure than that of the early church. As such there are issues that need to be considered at different levels of leadership while maintaining Paul's directive to be transparent with those in leadership (1

---

12. Kinnaman and Lyons, *Unchristian*, 53.
13. Erickson, *Christian Theology*, 578.

Tim 5:20). The text does say "elders"; however, the eldership in the contemporary church is a little more diverse than that of the early church.

The key to much of the success of the disciplinary process is the leadership of the church. Leadership tends to set the pace for the church. "Leadership is a dynamic process in which a man or woman with a God-given capacity influences a specific group of people toward His purposes for the group."[14] When sin puts this in jeopardy, the leadership of the church—not the entire community nor just the person in error—must provide biblical direction. Therefore, there needs to be a much more comprehensive approach to bring healing. The restoration of the people of God is first to bring them back into fellowship with God and then with each other. Restoration is the successful conclusion of the necessary activity of church discipline.

Heart of the Impact Zone

Those in the impact zone are all too often forgotten or neglected. The impact zone may be narrow or exceptionally broad depending on the person involved in the disciplinary process. The narrower the impact zone the more crucial the attention from the RCCT. Consider the following: the larger the impact zone, the more people that can provide care to each other. Conversely, the narrower the zone, the less people affected, the greater the opportunity for people to fall through the cracks. Especially in the family of the offender. As so much attention throughout the entire process is focused on the offender, close family members are side-lined in the shadows of the process.

The need for the care of the family may be less or greater depending on the nature of the offense. There are several steps that the RCCT can take to provide care for the family. Sandy Wilson, the wife of Dr. Earl Wilson, has several suggestions for providing support for the family of an offender. What they refer to as the RCCT (Restoration Critical Care Team) is called the Spiritual Care Team, but the two serve essentially the same purpose.

1. The Spiritual Care Team provides security for the children and spouse.
2. The Spiritual Care Team offered stability to all the family members during a time of great disruption.

---

14. Clinton, *The Making of a Leader*, 14.

3. The Spiritual Care Team gave support to the family.
4. The Spiritual Care Team provided a real spiritual challenge to our family.[15]

What needs to be taken away from this is the need to have attentive care for the family. Sandy also suggests a few additional points that would prove helpful for supporting the spouse in a chapter written by her. Even though Dr. Wilson's situation is specific to sexual impropriety, much of these support structures would benefit the family of any offender. While this should not by any means be restricted to family members of the clergy, special attention should be given in these situations. "Most people in our churches have no idea how demanding ministry can be or even how demanding they can be."[16]

As this discussion draws to a close, the one point that any reader should take away from it is this: regardless of the mess or the sin, where there is life there is hope. As long as the church does what only it can do, seek and save the lost, including those who have lost their way and surround them with the love of God in Christ, they can confront, repair, and restore, taking part in the building of the spiritual house that Peter envisioned. Mentioned earlier is an account of an offender from a church that ended well, with the sin confessed and the saint in restoration. This is not always the case. One last account, as the discussion draws to a close, is of a situation that went horribly wrong. An account that left many lives deeply damaged, some possibly permanently scarred, the offender unrepentant and those in the impact zone shattered.

Cassy's Story

Many stories in discussions such as this one are fictional, perhaps with elements drawn from real life. The two accounts in this discussion are both true and were chosen for two specific reasons. The first is an encouragement when things turn out for the good. The latter is a warning, what happens when the situation is not handled well and does not end well. This latter account is provided by a young lady named Cassy (not her real name), with the hope that reflection on it will cause others to take different routes and save some the pain that she and her family endured.

15. Wilson et al., *Restoring the Fallen*, 110.
16. Cordeiro, *Leading On Empty*, 33.

Cassy's father was the pastor of a small to mid-sized church that he had been pastoring for quite some time. He is described by Cassy as a tender-hearted and compassionate minister at the time when this situation developed. The first signs of trouble were detected by the pastor's wife who brought it to light. What she found was evidence that her husband had been engaged in an illicit affair through an online venue. The pastor had been taking steps to distance himself from the ministry, by beginning to fill his pulpit with special speakers. Wrapping up his ministry, the pastor eventually turned in his credentials and resigned. There had been no formal investigation. As soon as the situation was discovered, the pastor was ready to withdraw from both his ministry and his family. Therefore, no disciplinary action was pursued.

In an attempt to resolve this matter, another pastor was sent to deal with the fallout. Cassy laments that no one from the denominational office that the church represented showed up to the meeting that was held to deal with the issue. Many of those in attendance are reported to have not attended the assembly anywhere from three to four months to years, yet they were willing to come out and to assault the fallen. Cassy's entire family was required to attend—outside of her father. She reports that one by one people stood up and belittled the person, efforts, and ministry of her father. The pastor's entire family could do nothing but sit there and endure the spectacle. Cassy remembers sitting there so hurt and angered that all she could do was shake. No one made any attempt to close or control the meeting, including the pastor who had been dispatched from a substantial distance, until one of the neighbors of the pastor's family stood up and brought the meeting to a close.

In the aftermath of the meeting, some counseling was offered to members of the church but there was no care provided to those in the immediate center of the impact zone, the family! The wife of the offending pastor was abandoned by those she needed most. From the description provided by Cassy, the wife, ill and destitute, with no source of income, fell into a major depressive episode. Although the entire family was in desperate need of specialized care, none was offered. Cassy, the eldest, yet young, and a new mom, along with her husband, was the only one left to pick up the pieces for the entire family. No one from the church offered to help her mother and still-at-home sibling move when they were ousted from the parsonage. It was her non-Christian friends that saw the need and stepped in to help with the move. Cassy did her utmost to help them survive. The church that should have been there was not. Members of the family of God that should have been there were not. The denominational support that should have been there was not. Interactions with church members were less then positive. When former church members were not avoiding the family like the plague, they would unload more venomous accusations on the family members concerning their former pastor.

What should have happened? As soon as the church became aware of the situation, the elders should have met with the pastor, to offer guidance and support while at the same time to rebuke him for the situation. Denominational officers should have, upon notification, sent out some form of representative, to meet with the pastor and to counsel and support the church and the pastor's family. The gathering of the RCCT should have, upon hearing of the pastor's resistance to repentance, set out to minister to the family. The meeting to discuss the issue with the church should have been directed from the pulpit, not the pew. Guidance and admonition to the church should have been provided, concerning rumors, gossip, and what it means to be a people of grace. The meeting should have been centered upon praying for the pastor, to forsake his current course and return to fellowship. The meeting could have ended with the church gathered around a broken, vulnerable, and desperate family, to assure and love them. The healing hands of the Savior could have been extended through everyone as an extension of the Comforter. Let us take note and endeavor to do better.

Appendix A

BY-LAW 6—Discipline and Restoration[1]

1.1 **Nature and Purposes of Discipline:** Discipline is an exercise of scriptural authority for which the local church is responsible. The aims of discipline are that God may be honored, that the purity and welfare of the local church may be maintained, and that those under discipline may be brought to repentance and restoration.

Discipline is to be administered for the restoration of local church members, while fully providing for the protection and advancement of the spiritual welfare of our local churches. It is to be redemptive in nature as well as corrective and is to be exercised as under a dispensation of both justice and mercy. The following shall be proceeded with only after all other avenues of Christian counsel and brotherly admonition have been attempted.

1.2 **Causes of Disciplinary Action:** Any proven act or conduct which, in the opinion of the Board, after a full investigation of the evidence may be determined to be in contradiction of the actions and principles as stated in Article 6.1 of the "Local Church Constitution and By-Laws" may give just cause for disciplinary action by the Board. Without limiting the generality of the foregoing, among such causes for action shall be:

    1.2.1 Any moral failure involving sexual misconduct or sexual deviation (including, but not limited to adultery, homosexuality, incest, sexual assault, pornography, and improper contact with the opposite sex).

---

1. From Pentecostal Assemblies of Canada, "Local Church Consitution and By-Laws."

- **1.2.2** Any moral or ethical failure other than sexual misconduct or any conduct unbecoming to a local church member (including, but not limited to deception, fraud, theft, and assault).

- **1.2.3** Any act or action of a local church member, which is the cause of serious discord or dissension, with or without malicious intent (Rom 16:17, 18; Prov 6:19).

- **1.2.4** The propagation of doctrines and practices contrary to those set forth in the *Statement of Fundamental and Essential Truths* of The Pentecostal Assemblies of Canada.

1.3 Initiative

- **1.3.1 Authority:** Occasions sometimes arise which make it necessary to deal with local church members who have reached the place where, in the opinion of the Board, endorsement can no longer be given. The Board, which has the authority to approve church membership, also has the right to withdraw their approval and to dismiss church membership.

- **1.3.2 Board Responsibility:** The Board is responsible to deal with allegations of misconduct according to the *Local church Constitution and By-Laws*.

  In the event that the Board finds itself compromised in any manner, or appearing to lack impartiality, it shall have the right to appoint a substitute committee to hear charges against a church member.

- **1.3.3 Statement of Conduct:** Should a local church member admit to or confess to a wrongdoing or misconduct to the Board, such as should require disciplinary action, then the Board shall exercise discretion as to the appropriate form of discipline.

  Reports, Rumors, or Complaints: Should there be reports, rumors, or complaints, written or unwritten, which appear to be persistent, serious, becoming publicly known, and posing a detriment to the testimony of the individual or church, then the pastor shall use their judgment to discuss the matter with the member being accused, always in the presence of a member of the Board. The pastor and Board member shall exercise their discretion as to whether or not to commence an official investigation.

1.3.4 Investigation of Reports or Complaints of Alleged Violations: Written and signed allegations of violations under By-Law 6.2 by a local church member shall be investigated. The pastor shall appoint two (2) members of the Board to investigate the allegation, having in mind that it is their responsibility to safeguard the member, the local church, and the fellowship. This shall be done to determine the credibility of the allegation.

    1.3.4.1 Signed written allegations shall be filed with the Pastor and/or a member of the Board, by the complainant(s) describing the alleged violations.

    1.3.4.2 The persons making the allegation shall be interviewed in order to ascertain the facts in the case and the reasons underlying the allegation.

    1.3.4.3 The accused local church member shall be given an opportunity to be interviewed to discuss the allegation.

    1.3.4.4 Should a local church member, when presented with the allegations, acknowledge a wrongdoing that requires disciplinary action, then the Pastor or the Pastor's designate shall report the acknowledgment of wrongdoing to the Board who shall initiate appropriate disciplinary action and a restoration program.

    1.3.4.5 Should the local church member deny the allegations made, the investigators shall determine if the evidence merits a disciplinary hearing.

    1.3.4.6 Where an accused local church member serves in a leadership capacity in the local church, such ministry may be restricted during the investigation at the discretion of the Pastor.

1.3.5 Legal Charges

1.3.5.1 Where a local church member has been legally charged under the *Criminal Code* of Canada:

No disciplinary procedures will be followed until the legal proceedings, including appeal, have run their course.

Continuing involvement in the local church leadership may be subject to restriction during the time of the legal proceedings at the discretion of the Board.

1.3.5.1.1 A guilty verdict of a local church member following the legal proceedings, including appeal, shall automatically precipitate disciplinary procedures by the Board.

Local church members may be eligible for participation in a restoration program upon request for reconciliation.

1.3.5.2 Should the allegations against the local church member be one of a violation which is required by law to be reported (including, but not limited to, offences against minors), the Board shall report the accused to the appropriate legal authorities and delay their own investigation, until the appropriate legal authorities have opportunity to investigate.

1.3.6 **Preparation and Filing of Charges:** Allegations shall only be investigated when they have been made in writing, dated, and signed by the complainant.

If, after due investigation, it is determined that a disciplinary hearing should occur, charges should be filed with the Board.

The person against whom charges have been filed shall be informed by registered mail of the charges at least fifteen days before being called to appear before the Board for a disciplinary hearing. The hearing shall take place within forty days of formal charges being delivered to the local church member, or the entire proceeding shall be rescinded. A copy of the charges shall be sent to the District Superintendent.

The said local church member may be relieved immediately from local church involvement upon being notified of the charges.

1.3.7 **Disposition of Allegations**

    1.3.7.1 If written allegations are made and signed, but the investigators conclude under the guidelines of the *Local church Constitution and By-Laws* that no reason exists for a hearing, then the matter shall be dropped.

    1.3.7.2 The pastor, or the pastor's appointee, may seek to counsel all parties involved and to bring to an end any continuation of rumors or conflicts related to the matter.

    1.3.7.3 The complainant shall be informed in writing that the investigation has been concluded and the allegations dismissed.

    1.3.7.4 There shall be no record of the investigation kept.

    1.3.7.5 The church member shall be informed in writing that the investigation of the allegations has concluded, and no charges have been laid.

1.3.8 **Disciplinary Hearing:** In the event the investigators find the charges merit a hearing they shall request the pastor to arrange for a disciplinary hearing by the Board for the accused local church member. The local church member shall be requested to appear at the hearing.

To ensure the ability of the hearing committee to render an impartial judgment, no member of the Board of the local church may sit on the hearing committee when they have been party to the details of the investigation or any event or incident related to the alleged offence.

The pastor may attend the hearing as an observer but shall not participate nor be present when a vote is taken in the decision as to guilt or innocence. The role of the pastor is to be redemptive to all parties involved.

If the accused local church member refuses to appear at the hearing to offer a defence, the hearing will proceed, and the accused member may be disciplined if found guilty of the charges preferred.

1.3.8.1 Chair: A member of the hearing committee shall be appointed by the pastor to serve as chair.

The chair of the hearing committee along with the pastor shall prepare an agenda and arrange for all matters of the hearing.

The chair shall appoint a recording secretary from the membership of the hearing committee.

1.3.8.2 Role of Investigators

1.3.8.2.1 The investigators shall bring a report to the hearing and offer evidence as discovered during the investigation procedures.

1.3.8.2.2 They shall not participate nor be present when a vote is taken in the decision as to guilt or innocence.

1.3.8.2.3 No evidence or comment regarding the evidence shall be given by the investigators or accusers in the absence of the accused local church member, unless the accused local church member has failed to, or has refused to, appear at the hearing.

1.3.8.3 LOCAL church Member's Support: The accused local church member shall have the right to have a member of this local church present for support but not as an active participant in the hearing process. The supporting person may be the spouse of the accused local church member.

Legal counsel shall not be present for either side at the hearing.

1.3.8.4 The agenda and proceedings shall provide sufficient opportunity for the complainant and complainee to speak, offer evidence, cross examine, present witnesses, and to make a summation statement. It will be the role of the hearing committee to question and make inquiry of the participants and to seek to have all the facts, evidence, and testimony duly presented and examined to ensure an objective decision.

1.3.8.5 The verdict shall be made by secret ballot in the absence of investigators, the complainant, and the supporting member if present and the complainee. A two-thirds (2/3) majority vote shall be required to determine guilt.

1.3.8.6 If it has been determined that guilt has been established, discipline shall be administered prayerfully and in the fear of God, in accordance with the Scriptures and as set forth in the *Local church Constitution and By-Laws*.

1.3.8.7 Announcement of the Verdict

1.3.8.7.1 The verdict shall be communicated to the pastor and placed in the minutes of the Board. If the verdict is one of guilt, then the minutes of the hearing and any other relevant documents shall be maintained in a confidential file until the disciplinary process has been completed.

> **1.3.8.7.2** The pastor shall communicate the verdict in writing to the local church member and the complainant within five (5) days of the decision of the hearing committee.
>
> **1.3.8.7.3** If a guilty verdict is reached, the local church member shall be informed in writing of the right and process of appeal.
>
> If the verdict is one of not guilty, then no record of the hearing shall be maintained.

1.3.9 Discipline: A local church member who has been found guilty of violating or who has confessed in writing to having violated any of the principles set forth in the *Local church Constitution and By-Laws*, shall be subject to disciplinary action by the Board. Said discipline shall be administered in brotherly love and kindness. The Board shall weigh decisions on the basis of the offence itself.

A local church member who has confessed to, or been found guilty of, the charges may have their membership placed on probation, or suspended.

A local church member who refuses to enter the restoration program and does not complete the same shall have their membership dismissed.

1.3.10 Right of Appeal: The local church member shall have the right of appeal. The purpose of the appeal is to examine the process and the judgment rendered.

Any appeal of the decision by the hearing committee must be made in writing within thirty days of receiving the decision of the committee to the secretary of the Board. The Board shall request the District Superintendent to appoint a committee to hear the appeal.

The appeal will be heard within sixty days of receiving the request for an appeal in writing.

APPENDIX A: BY-LAW 6—DISCIPLINE AND RESTORATION

The accused person will be present at this appeal, but if the accused person neglects or refuses to attend the hearing, it may proceed in the absence of the accused person. The decision of this appeal committee will be final.

The decision of the appeal committee will be communicated in writing to the church member by the chair of the appeal committee within five (5) days of the appeal hearing.

Legal counsel shall not be present for either side at the appeal hearing, nor in any other investigative or disciplinary hearing provided for in these by-laws.

If the church member has chosen to not attend the hearing, then the member will not be eligible to appeal the decision that has been rendered.

1.3.11 Restoration: In the event a local church member who has been found guilty of offence shows repentance and indicates a desire for continued fellowship with the local church, the Board shall determine an appropriate restoration program, which would have in view the completion of a suspension period or the reinstatement of membership as applicable.

The program of restoration shall be administered in brotherly love and kindness.

The restoration program may include limitations of ministry involvement during the term of restoration.

1.3.12 Reinstatement of Membership: Persons who have had their membership suspended and have successfully completed the restoration program may apply for reinstatement of membership by communicating their request to the secretary of the Board.

1.3.13 Waiver of Claim: Notwithstanding the provisions hereinbefore contained, certificates of membership of this local church shall be issued upon the condition that suspension of the member and withdrawal of the certificate of membership in the manner herein provided shall not give the suspended member cause for legal action against the pastor or any member taking part in the suspension proceedings; and the acceptance of the certificate of membership or fellowship in this local church shall be evidence of a waiver by the member of all rights of action, causes of action, and all claims and demands against the local church or any member or officer of The Pentecostal Assemblies of Canada by virtue of suspension proceedings and withdrawal of the certificate of membership or fellowship in this local church under the foregoing provision.

APPENDIX B

RCCT Confidentiality Agreement

Guiding Principles:

1. Confidentiality is important in establishing and maintaining and lasting relationships among those who work to rebuild the lives of those needing care.
2. Confidentiality is the cornerstone to ensuring that privileged information is accessible only to those authorized to have access.
3. Confidentiality acknowledges respect for an individual's right to privacy.
4. Confidentiality assumes that those who pledge to safeguard confidential information will do so.
5. When using open/shared space (staff rooms, hallways, cubicles, etc.) privileged information that may be inadvertently shared or overheard is respected and kept confidential.

As an RCCT Member, I will receive and have access to confidential information about individuals, children, families, and ministries of this assembly. Except when required by law, this information will be kept in the strictest confidence.

I understand that the discussion, including electronic exchanges such as but not restricted to email and texts, of personal information about individuals, children, families, and ministry leaders without authorized consent is unethical.

APPENDIX B: RCCT CONFIDENTIALITY AGREEMENT

I will abide by this Confidentiality Agreement to ensure respect for the privacy of the individuals, children, families, and ministries at Squamish Community church.

Name of RCCT Member (Please Print)   Signature of RCCT Member

_____

Witness   Date (YY/MM/DD)

About the Author

Rev. Dr. James Kelly was born in Windsor, Ontario, Canada, son of John and Elizabeth Kelly, on March 25, 1963. He has one older half-sister and one older full sister.

Rev. Dr. Kelly was educated through the Separate (Catholic) School System in Calgary, Alberta, Canada. He attended undergraduate studies at Summit Pacific College in Abbotsford, British Columbia, from which he graduated with a Bachelor of Theology degree. Upon completion of his undergraduate studies he attended Regent College in Vancouver, British Columbia, Canada, graduating with a Master of Divinity degree.

Following his studies at Summit and during his studies at Regent he served in a number of cross-cultural and multicultural churches in the Lower Mainland of British Columbia. In April of 2004 he was called to serve in his previous assignment, in Squamish, British Columbia. During the time of his ministry the church has stabilized, began to heal some of the wounds of the past, and has restored confidence in the pastoral office.

Rev. Dr. Kelly is married to the former Christine Marie Malina. They have two children together who work extensively to assist their parent's growth in grace.

Bibliography

Adams, Jay E. *Handbook of Church Discipline: A Right and Privilege of Every Church Member.* The Jay Adams Library. Grand Rapids: Zondervan, 1986.
"Addiction." *Psychology Today.* https://www.psychologytoday.com/basics/addiction.
Alford, Henry. *Alford's Greek Testament: An Exegetical and Critical Commentary.* 8 vols. Grand Rapids: Guardian, 1976.
American Psychiatric Association. *Diagnostic and Statistical Manual of Mental Disorders: DSM-IV.* 4th ed. Washington, DC: American Psychiatric Association, 1994.
American Psychological Association. "Addictions." Accessed March 6, 2018. http://www.apa.org/topics/addiction/index.aspx.
———. "Trauma." Accessed March 6, 2018. http://www.apa.org/topics/trauma/index.aspx.
Arndt, William F., et al., eds. *A Greek-English Lexicon of the New Testament and Other Early Christian Literature.* Chicago: University of Chicago Press, 2000.
Balz, Horst, and Gerhard Schneider, eds. *Exegetical Dictionary of the New Testament.* 3 vols. Grand Rapids: Eerdmans, 1990–93.
Bargerhuff, Eric J. *Love That Rescues, God's Fatherly Love in the Practice of Church Discipline.* Eugene, OR: Wipf & Stock, 2010.
Barrett, C. K. *The First Epistle to the Corinthians.* Black's New Testament Commentary 7. Peabody, MA: Hendrickson, 1993.
Bayer, Oswald. *Living by Faith: Justification and Sanctification.* Lutheran Quarterly Books. Minneapolis: Fortress, 2017.
Beale, G. K., and D. A. Carson, eds. *Commentary on the New Testament Use of the Old Testament.* Grand Rapids: Baker Academic, 2007.
Blackaby, Henry T., and Richard Blackaby. *Spiritual Leadership: Moving People on to God's Agenda.* Rev. ed. Nashville: B&H, 2007.
Blocher, Henri. *Original Sin: Illuminating the Riddle.* New Studies in Biblical Theology. Grand Rapids: Eerdmans, 1999.
Blomberg, Craig L. *Matthew: An Exegetical and Theological Exposition of Holy Scripture.* New American Commentary 22. Nashville: Broadman, 1992.
Brown, Colin, ed. *The New International Dictionary of New Testament Theology.* 4 vols. Grand Rapids: Regency Reference Library, 1986.
Brown, Francis, et al. *Enhanced Brown-Driver-Briggs Hebrew and English Lexicon.* Oxford: Clarendon, 1977.

BIBLIOGRAPHY

Carson, D. A., et al., eds. *New Bible Commentary: 21st Century Edition*. 4th ed. Downers Grove, IL: InterVarsity, 1994.
Carter, Charles W., et al., eds. *A Contemporary Wesleyan Theology: Biblical, Systematic, and Practical*. 2 vols. Grand Rapids: Zondervan, 1984.
Chan, Francis, and Mark Beuving. *Multiply: Disciples Making Disciples*. Colorado Springs: David C. Cook, 2012.
Cheong, Robert K. *God Redeeming His Bride: A Handbook for Church Discipline*. Ross-Shire, UK: Christian Focus, 2012.
Clinton, J. Robert. *The Making of a Leader: Recognizing the Lessons and Stages of Leadership Development*. Colorado Springs: NavPress, 1988.
CogniFit. "Cognition and Cognitive Science." https://www.cognifit.com/cognition.
Cordeiro, Wayne. *Leading On Empty: Refilling Your Tank and Renewing Your Passion*. Bloomington, MN: Bethany House, 2009.
Corey, Gerald. *Theory and Practice of Counseling and Psychotherapy*. 10th ed. Boston: Cengage, 2016.
Davidson, Benjamin. *The Analytical Hebrew and Chaldee Lexicon*. Rev. ed. Peabody, MA: Hendrickson, 1981.
Egan, Gerard. *The Skilled Helper: A Problem-Management and Opportunity-Development Approach to Helping*. 7th ed. Pacific Grove, CA: Brooks/Cole, 2002.
Encyclopædia Britannica. "Homosexuality." https://www.britannica.com/topic/homosexuality.
Erickson, Millard J. *Christian Theology*. 3rd ed. Grand Rapids: Baker Academic, 2013.
Fee, Gordon D. *The First Epistle to the Corinthians*. Rev. ed. New International Commentary on the New Testament. Grand Rapids: Eerdmans, 2014.
Firefly. Season 1, episode 14, "The Message." Directed by Tim Minear. Aired July 28, 2003, on Fox.
Fox, Michael V. *Ecclesiastes*. JPS Bible Commentary. Philadelphia: Jewish Publication Society, 2004.
France, R. T. "Matthew." In *New Bible Commentary: 21st Century Edition*, edited by D. A. Carson et al. 4th ed. Downers Grove, IL: InterVarsity, 1994.
Friberg, Timothy, et al. *Analytical Lexicon of the Greek New Testament*. Baker's Greek New Testament Library. Grand Rapids: Baker, 2000.
George, Timothy. *Galatians: An Exegetical and Theological Exposition of Holy Scripture*. The New American Commentary 30. Nashville: Holman, 1994.
Grenz, Stanley J., and Roy D. Bell. *Betrayal of Trust: Sexual Misconduct in the Pastorate*. Downers Grove, IL: InterVarsity, 1995.
Hammett, John S., and Benjamin L. Merkle, eds. *Those Who Must Give an Account: A Study of Church Membership and Church Discipline*. Nashville: B&H, 2012.
Hudson, Ralph E. "A Glorious Church." Timeless Truths. http://library.timelesstruths.org/music/A_Glorious_church/.
Jamieson, Robert, et al. *Commentary Critical and Explanatory on the Whole Bible*. Oak Harbor, WA: Logos, 1997.
"Jealousy." *Psychology Today*. https://www.psychologytoday.com/basics/jealousy.
Jeschke, Marlin. *Discipling the Brother*. Harrisonburg, VA: Herald, 1972.
Kelly, J. N. D. *The Pastoral Epistles*. Black's New Testament Commentary 14. Peabody, MA: Hendrickson, 1993.
Kinnaman, David, and Gabe Lyons. *Unchristian: What a New Generation Really Thinks About Christianity . . . and Why It Matters*. Grand Rapids: Baker, 2007.

BIBLIOGRAPHY

Laney, J. Carl. *A Guide to Church Discipline: God's Loving Plan for Restoring Believers to Fellowship with Himself and with the Body of Christ.* Eugene, OR: Wipf & Stock, 2010.

Lange, John Peter. *Lange's Commentary on the Holy Scriptures: 1 & 2 Corinthians.* Grand Rapis: Zondervan, 1957.

Lauterbach, Mark. *The Transforming Community: The Practise of the Gospel in Church Discipline.* Rev. ed. Ross-shire, UK: Christian Focus, 2003.

Leeman, Jonathan. *Church Discipline: How the Church Protects the Name of Jesus.* 9Marks Building Healthy Churches. Wheaton, IL: Crossway, 2012.

———. *Church Membership: How the World Knows Who Represents Jesus.* 9Marks Building Healthy Churches. Wheaton, IL: Crossway, 2012.

Liddell, H. G., and R. Scott. *Greek-English Lexicon.* 9th ed. Oxford: Clarendon, 1996.

Louw, Johannes P., and Eugene Albert Nida. *Greek-English Lexicon of the New Testament: Based on Semantic Domains.* New York: United Bible Societies, 1996.

Lowery, David K. "1 Corinthians." In *The Bible Knowledge Commentary: An Exposition of the Scriptures*, edited by John F. Walvoord and Roy B. Zuck. Wheaton, IL: Victor, 1985.

Lukaszewski, Albert L., et al. *The Lexham Syntactic Greek New Testament, SBL Edition: Expansions and Annotations.* Bellingham, WA: Lexham, 2011.

Mare, W. Harold. *New Testament Background Commentary: A New Dictionary of Words, Phrases and Situations in Bible Order.* Ross-shire, UK: Mentor, 2004.

McRay, Barret W., et al. *The Modern Psychopathologies: A Comprehensive Christian Appraisal.* Christian Association for Psychological Studies Books. Downers Grove, IL: InterVarsity, 2005.

Merritt, Jonathan. "Pornography: A Christian Crisis or overblown issue?" *Religion News Service*, January 20, 2016. https://religionnews.com/2016/01/20/christians-pornography-problem/.

Metzger, Bruce M. *A Textual Commentary on the Greek New Testament: A Companion Volume to the United Bible Societies' Greek New Testament (4th Rev. ed.).* London: United Bible Societies, 1994.

National Communication Association. "Transactional Model of Communication." https://www.natcom.org/transactionalmodel/.

Nicoll, W. Robertson, ed. *The Expositor's Greek Testament.* Vols. 1–3. London: Hodder & Stoughton, 1897.

Pentecostal Assemblies of Canada. "Local Church Consitution and By-Laws." 2016 General Conference. https://www.paoc.org/docs/default-source/church-toolbox/constitutions/2016/local-church-constitution-2016.pdf?sfvrsn=3f67196a_2.

Plantinga, Cornelius. *Not the Way It's Supposed to Be: A Breviary of Sin.* Grand Rapids: Eerdmans, 1995.

Promise Keepers. "The 7 Promises." https://promisekeepers.org/about/7-promises.

Rutter, Peter. *Sex in the Forbidden Zone: When Men in Power—Therapists, Doctors, Clergy, Teachers, and Others—Betray Women's Trust.* New York: HarperCollins, 1990.

Rydelnik, Michael, and Michael Vanlaningham, eds. *The Moody Bible Commentary: A One-Volume Commentary on the Whole Bible by the Faculty of Moody Bible Institute.* Chicago: Moody, 2014.

Smith, Gordon T. *On the Way: A Guide to Christian Spirituality.* Vancouver, BC: Regent College Publishing, 2005.

Spurgeon, Charles H. *The Gospel of the Kingdom: A Commentary on the Book of Matthew.* London: Passmore & Alabaster, 1893.

BIBLIOGRAPHY

Staton, Knofel. *Timothy–Philemon*. Standard Bible Studies. Cincinnati: Standard, 1988.

Stronstad, Roger. *A Pentecostal Biblical Theology: Turning Points in the Story of Redemption*. Cleveland: CPT, 2016

Stutzman, Robert. *An Exegetical Summary of Galatians*. 2nd ed. Dallas: SIL International, 2008.

Thompson, Will L. "Softly and Tenderly Jesus is Calling." 1880. https://hymnary.org/text/softly_and_tenderly_jesus_is_calling.

Trail, Ronald. *An Exegetical Summary of 1 Corinthians 1–9*. 2nd ed. Exegetical Summaries. Dallas: SIL International, 2008.

Ward-Henninger, Colin. "Olympics moment: Derek Redmond finishes 400m with dad in Barcelona." *CBS News*, August 4, 2016. https://www.cbsnews.com/news/olympics-moment-derek-redmond-finishes-400m-dad-barcelona/.

The Westminster Assembly. *The Shorter Catechism with Scripture Proofs*. Carlisle, PA: Banner of Truth, 1998.

Whitbourne, Susan Krauss. "It's a Fine Line between Narcissism and Egocentrism." *Psychology Today*, April 7, 2012.

Wiersbe, Warren W. *The Bible Exposition Commentary*. 6 vols. Wheaton, IL: Victor, 1996.

———. *Wiersbe's Expository Outlines of the New Testament: Chaptery-by-Chapter through the New Testament with One of Today's Most Respected Bible Teachers*. Colorado Springs: David C. Cook, 1993.

Wigram, George V. *The Analytical Greek Lexicon of the New Testament*. Peabody, MA: Hendrickson, 1983.

Williams, Mark, et al. *The Mindful Way through Depression: Freeing Yourself from Chronic Unhappiness*. New York: Guilford, 2007.

Wilson, Earl, et al. *Restoring the Fallen: A Team Approach to Caring, Confronting & Reconciling*. Downers Grove, IL: InterVarsity, 1997.

World Health Organization. "Suicide Data." http://www.who.int/mental_health/prevention/suicide/suicideprevent/en/.

Yantzi, Mark. *Sexual Offending and Restoration*. Restorative Justice Classics. Eugene, OR: Wipf & Stock, 2009.

Zodhiates, Spiros, ed. *The Complete Word Study Dictionary: New Testament*. Word Study Series. Chattanooga, TN: AMG, 2000.

www.ingramcontent.com/pod-product-compliance
Lightning Source LLC
Chambersburg PA
CBHW050828160426
43192CB00010B/1933